Sustainable Composting

Sustainable Composting

Case studies and guidelines for developing countries

Editor: Mansoor Ali

Contributors
Malcom Harper
Anjum Pervez
Jonathan Rouse
Silke Drescher
Chris Zurbrugg

Prepared in collaboration with SANDEC/EAWAG, Switzerland

Water, Engineering and Development Centre
Loughborough University
2004

Water, Engineering and Development Centre
Loughborough University
Leicestershire
LE11 3TU UK

© WEDC, Loughborough University, 2004

Editor: Mansoor Ali (2004)
Sustainable Composting: Case studies and guidelines for developing countries

A reference copy of this publication is also available online from:
http://www.lboro.ac.uk/wedc/

ISBN Paperback 1 84380 071 3

This document is an output from a project funded by the UK
Department for International Development (DFID)
for the benefit of low-income countries.
The views expressed are not necessarily those of DFID.

Designed and produced at WEDC
by Sue Plummer

List of boxes

List of figures

List of photographs

List of tables

Contents

Part 1: Introduction

Chapter 1 3
Background

Chapter 2 5
The context

Part 2: Case Studies

Chapter 3 15
Decentralized composting in India

Chapter 4 29
A composting business in India

Part 1: Introduction

Chapter 1

Background

Disposal of increasing quantities of urban solid waste is a major challenge for municipal authorities. Resources are short, although some authorities have made investments to improve efficiency of solid waste management systems. Such projects often take a top-down approach and very little attention is paid to the potential economic and environmental benefits of reducing waste through integrating the role of non-government recyclers.

In low-income countries, much inorganic waste (such as metals and glass) is recycled by the informal sector, while non-governmental organisations and the private sector take the lead in recycling the organic portion through composting[1]. However, much of the organic portion as well as other, value-less waste remains a major problem. This often constitutes more than half by weight of the total solid waste generated and requires costly removal and disposal. Frequently, the failure of under-resourced authorities to collect waste leads to unpleasant city conditions, and decomposing waste constitutes a serious health and environmental hazard.

WEDC conducted a DFID research project, 'Promoting Compost as a Business for Urban Poor' (R8063), from August 2001 to September 2003. Since the technology for composting is simple and described elsewhere, the project focused its attention on the management of composting activities. This document presents the key findings from the project in the form of guidelines developed from case studies. The guidelines are produced to help in planning and managing compost projects, and so maximize their benefits.

---

1. Composting is a process of converting the organic portion of solid waste into a humus-like product. The final product, which is inert, can be used as a soil conditioner or for landfill cover.

This project focuses on the recycling of organic (as opposed to inorganic) waste by composting. While many projects have looked into the technological aspects of composting, this project focuses on demand for compost and marketing in low-income countries.

Poverty reduction and environmental sustainability are two of the eight Millennium Development Goals (MDGs). The project contributes to both these goals. Sustainable compost projects will not only benefit the environment but will also create jobs. Therefore, the main beneficiaries of this project would be poor people in urban areas, as existing and potential employees of the compost projects. In some cases, the poor may also own and run their own enterprises as recyclers of organic waste. As waste is already a major source of livelihoods for the urban poor, this is a sound strategy for bringing sustainable benefits to this group.

Composting schemes in India, Bangladesh, Sri Lanka, Pakistan and Ethiopia were studied in the project. Composting is a large topic and composting projects in developing countries usually operate under a number of constraints. Furthermore, people involved in the planning and management of compost projects need expertise in a wide range of subjects.

Most of the failures in composting projects arise from a lack of attention at the planning stage in understanding the demand and marketing aspects. Hence, the emphasis of the analysis in this book is on 'demand and marketing'. Based on the literature review and preliminary field surveys, issues around marketing and demand are discussed in the next chapter. Case studies from India, Pakistan, Bangladesh and Sri Lanka are then described, presenting some good practices and lessons learnt. The final chapter is a set of recommendations on gauging demand and enhancing the marketing of compost projects. Finally, there is a comprehensive list of useful references.

Chapter 2

The context

Composting has been practised in rural areas for centuries. Farmers traditionally put agricultural and some animal waste on their fields. This is mainly seen as a means of enhancing the soil. Composting of urban waste has a different motivation, however. The main motivation is to reduce and recycle the waste, particularly comparatively low-value components of waste. Within the context of urban solid waste management, composting projects become more challenging. There is a different set of stakeholders and processes, involving communities, city governments, donors and the private sector. Some examples of composters include:

- Governments and local authorities: a means of reducing organic urban waste

- Universities: to develop new technologies or assess quality issues

- NGOs: to demonstrate waste management solutions and create employment opportunities

- Entrepreneurs: to try new ideas and make money.

Most of these projects are small in scale. They are designed to demonstrate how the problem of urban waste management can be resolved while at the same time an income can be generated. Donors willingly fund such projects, as environmental sustainability is often high on their agenda. Often these projects are considered as a model for employment creation or improved working conditions for the poor. In any large city of a low-income country one can find a number of such activities, some that are still operating and some that have failed. There is very little analysis available on what policymakers can learn from these projects and what other good practices and lessons are available for future entrepreneurs.

As an increasing number of composting activities are being established in low-income countries and the projects have many different objectives, there is a need to analyse these activities and identify issues. A literature review has been carried out in Ethiopia, India, Bangladesh and Sri Lanka. Preliminary visits were undertaken in India, Bangladesh and Sri Lanka. The literature review and preliminary visits identified the following key issues common in low-income countries.

2.1   Issues

A clear focus on the objective
Some of the perceived benefits of composting are that it is:

• A solution to waste management problems

• A method by which to reduce quantities of waste

• A way of converting organic matter to a safer and useful product

• A mechanism for recycling nutrients to enhance long-term soil fertility

• An income and employment generation opportunity for the poor

• A way of reducing environmental pollution

• A demonstration of the successful conversion of organic waste.

Ideally, a compost project should be able to achieve many of the above objectives. One of the problems with many composting projects in low-income countries is that they lack focus, which means they have too many goals and that it is difficult to monitor their success or impact.

The marketing of compost
Most compost projects are successful in producing compost. However, the sustainability of a commercial compost plant will depend on the successful and continuous sale of the compost. If large quantities of household waste are converted to compost, large markets are needed. The current known markets for compost seem fairly restricted to household gardeners, nurseries and organic farmers. The uses of compost are limited and the customer base still needs to be expanded through awareness building and identification of new uses. Compost is a commercial product. Quality and customer satisfaction are also important for effective marketing and sustained sales. In most cases data on compost quality is not available and markets are poorly understood. Trial runs are often not

undertaken properly and data are compared with compost produced elsewhere instead of what people are using at present. Quality is also important from safety and environmental perspectives.

Learning from past experience

There is a lack of information relating to what comprises sustainability and what is required to achieve it. Many cities have examples of failed composting projects but very little analysis is available on why they have failed.

High on the donor's agenda

In the last few years NGOs, community groups and the private sector have been successful in finding funding for compost programmes. The funders have agreed to fund the projects for a number of reasons mentioned above. Composting is not always so high on the agenda of local authorities as there are often more pressing waste management needs. Non-governmental organizations (NGOs) and community groups are often funded to initiate composting activities. In some cities, private sector companies have also initiated compost projects, investing their own funds. These are often at a disadvantage because they attract less grant money and are less likely to receive support from local authorities. Funding mechanisms are distorting the market and creating unequal competition.

Poor partnerships with governments

Partnerships or enabling policies, including cross-financing from the government, have been shown to be necessary for the financial success of projects. Generally there is poor partnership between the government and NGOs or the private sector in composting and a lack of subsidy. Mechanisms need to be put in place to enable composters to benefit from the savings they bring about for local authorities (i.e. lower transportation and disposal costs). Subsidies from the government in the form of land and payment per tonne of waste processed are important parts of the business.

Poor stakeholder partnership

Compost production requires expertise in waste management, the composting process and technologies, community management, and business and marketing skills. Compost activities are initiated and run by a variety of organizations, and most do not have all these skills. Some organizations, because of their nature, are good at waste processing, some at marketing of a product like compost and some at community campaigns.

Holistic approach

There is often a failure to take the overview of the situation, in the context of both waste management and the business environment. In some cases funders decide to pay for one part of a project while other details remain poorly defined and/or funded. For example, in one case household bins were provided without enough consideration of how the compost would be collected, used or sold. In other circumstances the source of raw organic waste may not be not properly considered.

Financial viability

Many compost projects are initiated for environmental or poverty alleviation reasons, but because they are not financially viable, they fail after some time. There is ultimately a need for composting projects to be designed and run in a financially viable way.

Choice of technology

Compost production uses different types of technologies to process the organic portion of waste, ranging from barrels and simple shredders to large windrow-turning machinery. These technologies are selected on the basis of a number of factors, for example the composter's capacity to operate and maintain, labour cost, power inputs, cost, production capacity, and the nature of the waste. The objective of the composting plant also affects choice: for example if employment generation is an objective then an operator may choose less technology and more labour intensive approaches. It should be possible for integrated systems to be developed which minimize adverse impacts on the poor whilst keeping productivity and efficiency high.

Barriers to home composting activities

When household based compost activities were introduced in some cases, the public motivation for using barrels and separation at source was initially low. Small sizes of plots, confusion over what to separate, and cultural reasons for not wishing to touch waste all restrict composting activities.

Co-operation from households is extremely important

Composting requires pure waste streams, and the best way to achieve this is by promoting household separation of waste. Householder co-operation depends on relationships between them, collectors and the composting organization, their attitudes and expectations, and levels of fees charged. If households are asked to pay fees for waste collection they like to know how the money is used and what income is derived from compost sales etc. Getting waste separated without a high level of environmental motivation or economic incentive is difficult to achieve. Awareness raising and 'community mobilization' are often found to be the most effective and sustainable means to get residents co-operating.

Composters rarely reap any benefits from the savings in waste disposal

There is usually no system by which savings to local authorities in terms of waste transportation and disposal are transferred to composters. This is because the motivation is not there from the authorities' side, because dumping is often highly unregulated in low income cities, and because municipalities are often severely underfunded so savings are not realized as 'spare cash'. There are, however, examples where composting communities have reaped benefits of savings to authorities by being given improved roads and sewers in their compound.

The urban poor have shown little interest in composting

In low income countries the urban poor are extensively involved in waste recycling so their lack of interest in composting begs an important question: Why? Often the poor are aware of what composting is and remember family members doing it in the past, but they are unaware of the technology, process or potential markets for the product. Financially viable compost projects could benefit the poor by providing employment and additional income as well as a cleaner local environment and improved soils. Other reasons for lack of composting activity among the poor may be that they do not have the necessary capital to enable them to begin making compost (including to buy or rent land), but also that composting is often found to be unprofitable.

Photograph 2.1. Non-compostable coconut shells at a plant in Sri Lanka.

Some organic waste requires shredding

Waste that is slow to biodegrade or large in size is not useful in its present form and it is necessary to shred it. This has time and cost implications. Shredders require power and cost money, and time to operate. This is a regional issue; for example, in Sri Lanka coconut husks are a big problem.

Business persons do not see composting as a business venture

Although there are examples of entrepreneurs investing in composting, there are often deeper environmental or social reasons for them wishing to do this which compensate for their acknowledgement that this is not a profitable activity.

Legal barriers to markets

Farmers and exporters of organically grown produce are potentially huge markets for compost, but are limited by the need for organic compost certification. The cost of certification and number of certificates required to open up different agricultural markets is a major barrier to poor, small-scale producers. This may point to the need for decentralized production but centralized distribution.

Costs of switching to organic fertilizer

There are other limitations to markets in the agricultural and organic farming sectors because of the high short-term costs. Farmers need to invest heavily in the first year of using compost to raise the quality of their soil, many normally rely on credit from the fertilizer suppliers, so this needs to be considered by compost suppliers.

The role of fertilizer distributors in marketing and distributing compost

In a number of places, fertilizer distributors are purchasing compost and selling it with their products, sometimes blended with fertilizers. This is a way of exploiting competition rather than competing, and will tend to make chemical fertilizer companies less threatened by organic farming. This is happening extensively in Bangladesh, not so much in Sri Lanka.

There is a need to understand workforce efficiency

Waste Concern Bangladesh employs 15 people to produce 3 tonnes per day of compost. Other places combine mechanization with labour because the cost of a labour-intensive system is too high. Businesses will always wish to run at optimum efficiency.

Employment creation and improved labour conditions are not guaranteed

Whereas an NGO may be setting up a composting plant with the interests of the poor in mind, a business may not have such concerns at heart. Therefore, many of the benefits that workers for NGOs enjoy (e.g. good working hours and conditions, good relations with managers, flexible attitude to needs) may not be assumed to be present in more business-oriented plants.

In many places waste work, including composting, is stigmatized

In Sri Lanka, it was reported that workers dislike working with waste as it is considered unpleasant and embarrassing. In Bangladesh, it was reported that workers at the Dhaka Waste Concern plant prefer it over garment work or being housemaids (the main alternatives open to them). However, a number of them lied about where they worked because they considered the work degrading. They told friends they worked in a 'factory'.

Land availability and cost

In Dhaka, shortage of land is a major problem. Authorities have proposed giving land to compost projects to prevent land being taken by squatters. The process of assigning land in Dhaka takes a number of years, and there are also questions around relative benefits to the poor: is this environmental improvement at the cost of housing areas for the poor? Also, so far, land has only been provided to NGOs: would authorities grant land to businesses for composting?

Location of composting sites is critical

If a choice is available, plants should be sited near the collection area, near a landfill site (for providing raw materials and dumping waste) or near the agricultural land or other market location. It would be possible to calculate optimum locations based on proximity to market, transportation costs, availability of labour and cost of land.

There is often resistance in low-income areas to home composting

Some reasons for people's resistance to home composting include lack of space, dislike of the smell or the flies that are attracted, impermanence of their homes and plots discouraging them from investing, and security (barrels can be stolen or sabotaged).

How we can ensure that the poor really benefit from composting

Get a project primarily financially sustainable but then ensure that workers are treated well and have sustainable and fair employment.

Part 2: Case Studies

Chapter 3

Decentralized composting in India

Silke Drescher and Christian Zurbrügg

EAWAG/SANDEC, P.O. Box 611, 8600 Dübendorf, Switzerland

This study was carried out as a part of the Department of Water and Sanitation in Developing Countries (SANDEC)'s Environmental Sanitation Research Programme. The project 'Decentralized Composting in India' aimed at assessing all relevant aspects of decentralized composting schemes, in order to set up recommendations for municipal stakeholders and interested individuals and groups.

The waste management situation in Indian cities was considered desperate in the late 1990s, with little hope for improvement in the near future. This gave rise to a public interest litigation filed in the Supreme Court of India. A committee constituted by the Supreme Court of India was then asked to look into all aspects of solid waste management and submit appropriate recommendations. On the basis of these recommendations (Committee Constituted by the Hon. Supreme Court of India 1999) the national legislation was adopted with the 'Municipal Solid Waste (Management & Handling) Rules 2000' (Ministry of Environment and Forests 2000). One section of the rules requires Urban Local Bodies to promote and implement waste segregation at source. The segregated 'wet' waste - the biodegradable organic fraction - has to be treated in an appropriate manner. With the existing legal backing, members of the community now have the means to force municipalities to take action.

All around India, various small-scale decentralized composting schemes are already operating with various levels of success. Often initiated by non-governmental organizations (NGOs), community-based organizations (CBOs), or motivated individuals, the experiences gained at these sites are extremely valuable for municipalities or other organizations and individuals interested in the management of organic waste.

Photograph 3.1. Shallow windrow composting at Sindh Colony, Pune. The scheme is very well protected from sight of residents and the roof protects the compost from being soaked during the rainy season. The compost is sold at Rs6/ kg to residents and neighbouring colonies.

This case study summarizes different approaches of decentralized composting schemes in the cities of Bangalore, Chennai, Pune and Mumbai. It provides information on their technical, operational, organizational, financial and social set-ups. For this case study the decentralized organizations include neighbourhood and community initiatives (by community-based organizations), company and institution initiatives for internal waste management, and private enterprises. Lessons learned from these composting experiences are briefly summarized below, but have also been documented and distributed to the Urban Local Bodies in India.

3.1 Why decentralized composting?

In the 1970s the interest in large-scale highly mechanized municipal solid waste (MSW) composting plants for urban areas grew worldwide. Most of these composting plants turned out to be serious financial failures (Dulac 2001). A study carried out in India (UNDP/WB RWSG-SA 1991) analysed 11 heavily subsidized mechanical municipal compost plants constructed between 1975 and 1985, ranging from 150 to 300 tonnes waste input capacity per day. The study concluded that in 1991 only three were in operating condition and that these plants were operating at much lower capacities than expected. The study recommended: 'Instead of setting up one single large mechanical compost plant, it will be beneficial to set up several small manual composting plants.'

In the 1990s many small-scale composting initiatives were initiated by NGOs or community groups, often receiving some international assistance and/or advice (Furedy no date). Some of these exist to date; others have disappeared after a few project years. However, decentralized composting schemes can be seen as promising management and treatment options for urban areas, as they:

- Enhance environmental awareness in a community

- Create employment in the neighbourhood

- Are more flexible in operation and management, adapting rapidly to changes in users' needs

- Are close to the residents, allowing close quality surveillance of the service and product

- Are based on labour-intensive technology and better adapted to the specific socio-economic situation

- Reduce waste management costs for the municipality as organic waste is diverted from the municipal waste stream, thereby reducing transportation and disposal costs

- When combined with primary collection services, can decrease dependence on malfunctioning municipal services.

3.2   Types of decentralized composting schemes

The composting schemes studied in India could be categorized according to their organizational set-up into:

- Neighbourhood initiatives and community-based waste collection and composting schemes

- Medium-scale private sector composting enterprises

- Initiatives of companies and institutions composting on their premises

- Public private partnerships in large-scale composting schemes.

With exception of the large-scale partnership composting schemes, all other types can be considered decentralized approaches as they treat waste collected from defined areas in a close radius of the composting plant. A more detailed description will provide interesting insights on the most typical technical, financial, organizational, and social factors of decentralized schemes.

Community-based schemes

Key common features of community-based schemes are:

- Their small scale of operation

- High degree of public participation

- Initiated by residents as a response to a crisis in waste management

- Primary waste collection service is mostly the core activity of the initiative for which residents pay fees.

Photograph 3.2. Composting bins at Kalyana Nagar Residents Association, Bangalore. The area is kept clean in order to avoid complaints from the neighbourhood. The compost is mainly sold to residents but also used for public gardens in the area.

The needs and priorities of the residents themselves set the framework of the scheme. Revenues by fee collection - a very tedious and time-consuming task, mostly conducted by voluntary members - often guarantees the financial viability of the scheme.

Table 3.1. Community-based initiatives, sorted by the number of households serviced

Name of scheme	Composting technique	Land space available (sq m)	No. of households serviced	Waste composted (kg/day)
Sandu Lane ALM, Mumbai	Bin composting	16	120	?
Diamond Garden Residents Forum (DGRF ALM), Mumbai	Bin composting	100	125	60
Scientific Handling of Waste Society (SHOW), Bangalore	Bin composting with active aeration	190	180	50
Sindh Colony, Pune	Shallow windrows	150	264	200
EXNORA Ramanathan, Chennai	Bin composting	40	300	300
Shyam Nagar Slum, Mumbai	Pit composting	60	350	350
Pammal, Chennai	Vermi-composting in bins	300	476	100
CEE Kalyana Nagar Residence Association, Bangalore	Bin composting	500	980	122
Residents Initiative for a Safe Environment (RISE), Bangalore	Bin composting	290	1200	300

An unreliable secondary collection service from the municipal authorities is often the main practical reason to start composting. The schemes rely on source-segregated waste. In some cases the waste collectors also sort mixed waste into different fractions during the collection process, as not all households in the collection area can be persuaded to segregate the biodegradable fraction. Some schemes have even adapted their collection vehicle to facilitate this activity. An acceptable level of household segregation is considered to be one of the key factors of successful schemes.

Most biodegradable waste is composted in bins or by vermi-composting (see Table 3.1).

Box 3.1. Advanced locality management, Mumbai

Mumbai Municipality has been successful in supporting neighbourhood schemes called Advanced Locality Management (ALM) with technical and organizational support addressing different aspects of urban life and sanitation. However, these support structures are still provisional and unfortunately are not yet institutionalized into the regular municipal functions. ALMs are formed on the basis of streets or other small areas and consist of community-based structures or neighbourhood initiatives, which are formally recognized and supported by the municipal authorities.

The municipality provides a platform for exchange and communication among ALM representatives and municipal authorities. These meetings enable the residents to convey their area-related problems such as waste collection, road repair, lighting, water supply or drainage problems in front of the municipal authorities. Initially waste collection and street sweeping are often the priority focus of ALMs. Composting activities usually follow at a later stage. Out of 670 ALMs in Mumbai, 284 have incorporated box-composting activities. The municipal target is to have at least one composting site per ward. Even if composting is not on the list of priorities for ALMs it is important to recognize that the institutionally embedded structure of the ALM system sets the framework for such possible future activities.

Photograph 3.3. Box system located at the Diamond Garden Residents Forum, treating the waste of 125 households. The compost produced is used for the greening of public places and as potting material. The bins are located above a drainage system at the former dumping area, which saves space. The neighbour appreciated the composting bins which replaced a smelly temporary dumping area.

It was observed that there is some confusion over the terminology concerning technological approaches as well as a general lack of scientific knowledge on the composting process. The term vermi-composting is very often used even when the number of worms contributing to the process is minimal and the resulting product did not consist of vermicastings (with the exception of Pammal, Chennai). Composting in bins, observed frequently, consists of filling the biodegradable fraction into brick-built bins constructed with aeration structures. Composting duration is approximately two to three months. Limited turning and watering was noted which reflects the limited technical knowledge of some schemes.

The compost produced is mainly sold in the neighbourhood, where marketing strategies are limited to word-of-mouth information by the collectors or core members of the associations. Scientific Handling of Waste Society (SHOW), an NGO in Bangalore, has also been able to target companies for compost use in their gardens and parks. Compost prices have a vast range from Rs6 in Pune up to Rs20/kg in Mumbai which also reflects the middle and high income users targeted in the areas where these schemes are often located.

The main challenges for the schemes are odour complaints by the nearby residents and the lack of municipal support and formal acknowledgement. Municipal support is often only limited to informal agreements of land provision for composting. Table 3.1 gives an overview of all the community-based composting schemes visited, considering their technique, size and capacity.

Medium-scale business oriented enterprises

These systems are run by individual entrepreneurs or NGOs, who have identified the organic waste treatment as a business opportunity and found a market for the end product. Entrepreneurs have invested private money in the business or taken loans. Banks consider investments in solid waste management projects as high-risk businesses due to a lack of experience and proven winners in this field. The high cost of land is a major obstacle for the set-up of a viable composting plant in urban areas. Therefore it is not surprising that many plants use municipal property which is provided free or at moderate rents.

The composting businesses observed do not use household wastes as feedstock. They all focus on 'pure organic' waste streams such as waste from vegetable, flower or fruit markets as well as residues from agro-industries. There is often already intense demand for these wastes, so the composting businesses have to compete for access to waste. Household waste is not preferred, as mixed waste sorting is too time-consuming and source segregation is not commonly practised.

Even though there is a potential for using segregated waste, awareness building and the implementation of such systems among households are too challenging and expensive for most of the private enterprises.

Table 3.2. Overview of small and medium size composting businesses visited

Name of scheme	Composting technique	Land space available (sq m)	Waste composted (kg/day)	Compost production (kg/ day)
Terra Firma, Bangalore	Windrow and vermi-composting	40 000	96 000	13 800
Vermigold at Dadar Pumping Station	Small windrows for vermi-composting	1 700	5 000	Not sold
Green Cross near Varsova Pumping Station	Shallow windrows	1 400	5 000	Unknown
Clean Air Island Composting Site at Colaba Pumping Station	Composting beds	760	5 000	Unknown

The assessed composting enterprises have difficulties in covering their costs through the sale of compost. This can be attributed to the difficult market situation but is also a result of weak marketing and sales strategies. With the exception of Terra Firma in Bangalore, which markets the compost through a large fertilizer distribution company, the schemes do not fully exploit the compost market. Three of the four schemes visited do not even have records of the amount of compost sold and could not tell the researchers the criteria that were used to select a market segment. For additional income some entrepreneurs act as consultants for associations or companies wanting to start composting activities or cross-subsidize the composting activities with the revenues from waste collection fees. Composting in India is still solely seen as a means of solid waste treatment, though it should be considered as a demand-driven activity addressing potential markets for compost.

Composting plants with a business approach provide job opportunities to low-income groups in India. Both male and female workers profit from the business; they are employed for waste collection, sorting, composting or as drivers. Middle-income groups with a higher education level also profit from such businesses, especially if they are run in a professional way. Secretaries,

Box 3.2. Vermigold Ecotech Pvt. Ltd., Mumbai

Vermigold is a vermi-composting company with five years' experience of providing mainly composting solutions to other organizations such as hotels, colleges, clubs and individuals, which are willing to compost their waste. Based on the premises of an old waste water treatment plant, they produce compost and worms in order to provide the material as starter and feedstock for new vermi-composting plants. They do not sell compost as fertilizer. The site is provided by the municipality at low rent. Vermigold does not get a collection fee for the market waste they collect for the scheme. The business is facing high risk as it is difficult to sell composting solutions regularly.

Photograph 3.4. Vermi-composting scheme at the Dadar Pumping Station, composting shredded market waste in small windrows

supervisors or accountants take over special duties in the whole process. In contrast to the small-scale plants, the jobs are more likely to be full time jobs and additional income from selling recyclable material is not sought.

Composting on institution and company premises

Systems and scales of operation that are chosen in these schemes are usually similar to the ones already mentioned. The systems mostly observed were bin composting in combination with vermi-composting or open pit composting.

Box 3.3. TATA Power Residents Colony, Mumbai

This corporate housing colony has 520 flats in a spacious well-wooded campus. Earlier, contractors were hired to collect the waste and dump it in municipal bins. After an enquiry and proposal from a waste-pickers co-operative, the colony changed the contractor. This women's initiative provided a significantly better service than the former contractor, however their knowledge about composting was limited. They sort the waste, sell recyclables, and compost the organic fraction on shallow beds on the campus premises. The compost remains on the campus as it cannot be sold in the Mumbai market. The initiative provides jobs to 18 women and two supervisors. The residents do not directly pay the collection fees but a residents association pays about Rs50,000 per month coming from rental fees. The shortfall of Rs15,000 is paid by a grant from the TATA Power Company.

Photograph 3.5. Pit composting at TATA Power Residents Colony, one of the least cost solutions for composting. Such systems are only feasible if plenty of space is available and residents live at a considerable distance, as odours can result from the uncontrolled composting process.

These schemes are set in a special organizational framework as they are initiated, controlled and managed by the institution or company in question. It is either the employees of the institution that operate the facilities themselves or else outside workers are contracted for this activity. The compost produced is mostly used on the premises and so does not need marketing. The decision to engage in composting results either from cost savings aspects or environmental consciousness. Cost factors can come into play where a company or institution has to pay the municipality for transport of waste from their premises to the landfill. Thus savings of collection and transport fees can be achieved by recycling and composting. Decisions on the 'if, how and when' of a recovery scheme are usually taken by the department in charge of environmental aspects of the organization. The advantages of such top-down set-ups are the relative ease and speed of decision-making as well as tight monitoring of a scheme. The participation of residents or employees is often minimal which in turn reflects in their environmental awareness.

From the employment point of view, it is often the urban poor that benefit through regular employment for collection and composting.

3.3   Conclusions

Examples of these community initiatives reveal some of the advantages of decentralized composting, such as the improved environmental conditions in residential areas. However, this also depends on a well functioning and regular primary waste collection. There is less waste to be collected by the municipality and an increased environmental awareness among residents: citizens welcome the positive changes in their immediate environment. Separate collection and composting of market wastes also contributes to reducing the environmental impacts at disposal sites. Nonetheless, decentralized composting cannot fully develop its effectiveness due to some critical prevailing operational and institutional issues.

The direct stakeholders involved in decentralized composting are recommended to reflect and improve on the following points in order to attain long-term feasibility and operational profitability.

Accounting and transparency

The data collected during the field study revealed a scarcity of documentation on mass flows and unclear financial figures. Numerous cases lack an information database and project planning is therefore not possible. Input-Output Tables for waste, compost and recyclables as well as monthly Cost-Revenue Balances would increase transparency and would also provide a sound basis for negotiations with the municipal authorities. Improved data documentation would thus increase the professional status of citizens' initiatives as well as junior companies.

Composting technique

Improvement measures are also required for most of the composting schemes, particularly to ensure a controlled composting process to prevent odour emissions and related complaints from nearby residents. During the field study, various competence centres for composting were identified for their important role in the dissemination of appropriate composting techniques (e.g. Institute of Natural Organic Agriculture or INORA, Pune).

Marketing

Development of adequate strategies and the identification of market segments for compost are the prerequisites for successful and long-term operation of decentralized composting. Nearly all enterprises examined lack an appropriate business plan including a marketing strategy. A timely assessment of different improvement options is required, such as direct marketing or the use of already available outlets of other contractors of agricultural products.

The role of municipal authorities

Common challenges for all decentralized composting schemes were identified that constrain the replication of such activities on city-wide level. A main common difficulty of all decentralized schemes is considered to be the lack of municipal acceptance and support.

Municipal support for decentralized schemes was observed to be limited to the provision of land, and, even these sites are usually allocated in an informal manner and do not give the composting schemes any legal backing. It is recommended that municipalities ensure:

- Political will and continuity of policy

- Development of action plans on how to ensure appropriate organic waste management

- Education and training of the entire MSW personnel

- Prompt and regular lifting of compost rejects (materials without recyclable value, currently especially thin polyethylene bags) from decentralized composting sites

- Encouragement of institutions, companies and citizens to take up composting

- Recruiting resource persons who can provide sound technical guidance on composting

- Buy-back arrangements and use of locally produced compost by the city authorities

- Promotion of and assistance with marketing activities for compost use in private gardens as well as for agricultural purposes

- Household segregation.

If there are financial profits from compost sales, they are small. Currently it does not seem possible to achieve 'gold from waste', as is sometimes stated. However, the increased interest of municipalities in organic waste management by composting, increased awareness on compost benefits, and developing markets for compost could significantly change the picture in the near future.

3.4   References and further reading

Committee Constituted by the Hon. Supreme Court of India, (1999). Solid waste management in Class I cities of India. Hon. Supreme Court of India, India.

Dulac, N., (2001). The organic waste flow in integrated sustainable waste management. A. Scheinberg, editor. Tools for Decision-makers -- Experiences from the Urban Waste Expertise Programme (1995-2001). WASTE, Nieuwehaven.

Furedy, C. (no date), Initiatives for Source Separation and Urban Organic Waste Reuse. Internet source: www.gdrc.org/uem/waste.

Ghosh, A., (1998). Management of Urban Environment - A Study on Post-Plague Initiatives of Surat Municipal Corporation. Urban Studies Department, Institute of Social Sciences, Delhi.

Ministry of Environment and Forests, (2000). Municipal Solid Wastes (Management and Handling) Rules 2000. The Gazette of India, New Delhi.

Rajagopal, K., (1998) India's Environment Pollution and Protection. Report No. 97ED57, Submitted to Central Research Institute of Electric Power Industry (CRIEPI, Japan). Tata Energy Research Institute (TERI), New Delhi, http://www.teriin.org/reports/rep01/rep01.htm.

UNDP/WB RWSG-SA, (1991). Indian experience on composting as means of resource recovery. UNDP/WB Water Supply and Sanitation Program South Asia, Workshop on Waste Management Policies, Singapore 1-5 July 1991, India.

Chapter 4

A composting business in India

Malcolm Harper (editor)

4.1   The origins of the business

M.K. Bhalerao lives in Saoner, a small town of some 27,000 people about thirty kilometres from the city of Nagpur, in Maharashtra. Mr Bhalerao had worked in the nearby Ballarpur Paper Mills for 32 years, as manager of the feedstock preparation plant, and was therefore familiar with the practical aspects of the chemistry of bulk organic materials and their treatment.

Like many retired people, Mr Bhalerao wanted to give something back to society after he had finished full-time employment. He involved himself in some local social work, but he felt that the results were not particularly satisfactory, so he decided that he would occupy himself with farming. He bought a small four hectare (ten acre) farm on the outskirts of the town, but he soon found that the place suffered from a major disadvantage, which totally destroyed any pleasure he might have gained from the work.

Threats and opportunities

Like most local authorities in India and other poorer countries, the Saoner municipality coped with the problem of solid waste by having it transported in trolleys and dumped on the outskirts of the town, with no further processing. Mr Bhalarao's home and farm are very close to the waste dumping ground, and this caused major problems. The accumulated waste could be smelled all around, it attracted flies and scavenger dogs, it polluted the groundwater and it made the surrounding areas almost uninhabitable.

Mr Bhalerao decided that this problem might actually be an opportunity for him to make good use of the knowledge he had gained in his work in the paper mill, and to achieve some of the social objectives which he had always had in mind to work for after his retirement from full-time employment. By solving the problem he might be able to contribute to the improvement of the environment, to provide employment for some of the large numbers of unemployed in the area, to improve the fertility of his own and other farmers' land and to occupy himself profitably. Composting seemed to offer a 'win-win' solution for all concerned.

Mr Bhalerao decided to undertake a small-scale experiment. He separated out some of the organic material from the rubbish at the dump, and transported it to his farm. He allowed it to stand for some time, and did what he thought was necessary to make it into usable compost, but the resulting material lacked many of the chemical components which are needed to make it into an effective composting medium.

Business potential

He determined to find out more. He studied some books on the subject, and went to an exhibition organized by the Excel Company, India's major manufacturer of composting equipment, and also a major supplier of finished compost. He spoke to the company's experts, and read through their technical material, and thus realized the mistakes he had been making. He also saw that there was a big potential market for good quality compost; the Excel brand was sold at a retail price of Rs5000, or $100, per tonne.

In January 1999, therefore, he determined to start a full-scale business to manufacture and market compost. He named it Anamol Krishi Udyog (Amol's Society Business) and chose the brand name 'Bhoosampda' for its product.

He made some enquiries about the waste situation in Saoner. He found that the town generates eight tonnes of solid waste every day, of which some five tonnes is from households, and a further three tonnes is generated from the local vegetable market. The Saoner area grows large quantities of vegetables. Much of this production passes through the market in Saoner town, and this generates a large amount of vegetable waste. More than 70 per cent of the solid waste is organic, from which good quality compost can be produced.

Mr Bhalerao prepared a project proposal for his business to convert the waste into compost, and submitted it to the municipal council members in Saoner. The Council agreed to the suggestion, and they passed a resolution awarding him a five-year contract to process the town's organic solid waste. He agreed to pay a royalty of $100 per year to the municipality. In return for this, he was allowed to operate his business on part of the dumping site, and the municipality agreed to collect and deliver all the town's waste to the site, which is of course quite close to Mr Bhalerao's own farm.

4.2   The process

The agreement did not include the supply of water or electricity at the dumping site, since funds were not available for this. Mr Bhalerao therefore arranged to pipe the sewage water from some fifteen to twenty nearby households to a nearby pond. This was in turn pumped to the composting site with an electric pump which was operated with power drawn from the supply to Mr Bhalerao's house. The organic material in the sewage water also serves to enrich the compost.

After the non-organic material has been separated out from the mixed waste which has been dumped by the municipality, the remaining organic waste is neatly piled in small heaps. Water is sprinkled on to these heaps and a moisture content of between 25 and 30 per cent is maintained for the rest of the process. After the first watering, one kilogram of a proprietary biological conversion agent is added for each tonne of organic waste. One gram of this conversion agent contains approximately eighty million micro-organisms; if the correct moisture content and temperature are maintained, these multiply by three every two hours, and this significantly increases the rate at which the solid waste is broken down and converted into usable compost.

The temperature of the heaped material rises to approximately 70° C after seven days, because of the heat generated from the biological reaction. At this point the material is aerated. The heaps are turned over, and this process is repeated every seven days. The moisture content and internal temperature of the heaps are constantly monitored.

After the digestion and conversion process is complete, the composted material is spread out for drying in the sun. The moisture content is reduced to 25 per cent, and then the material is passed through sieves to produce granules of a uniform size. Finally, the completed compost is packed into 40kg bags and is stored in the nearby warehouse ready for sale. The digestion process significantly reduces the weight and bulk of the raw material, and it takes about three tonnes of raw organic waste to produce one tonne of finished compost.

The chemical analysis of Bhoosampda compost is shown in Table 4.1.

Table 4.1. Components of 'Bhoosampda' organic compost[1]

Component	Content
Organic carbon	20-25%
C:N ratio	12-15
Nitrogen (N)	1.2-1.5%
Phosphorus (P)	1.2-1.5%
Potassium (K)	0.8-1.0%
Calcium (Ca)	1.0-1.3%
Magnesium (Mg)	0.3-0.5%
Sulphur (S)	0.2-0.3%
Zinc (Zn)	30-60 ppm
Iron (Fe)	300-500 ppm
Manganese (Mn)	200-400 ppm
Copper (Cu)	30-40 ppm
Boron (B)	10-50 ppm
Molybdenum (Mo)	40-50 ppm
pH (1:10 water extract)	8.26
EC (1:10 Wat. ext.) mmho/cm	4.92

1. This analysis was prepared by Ranadey Analabs Pvt. Ltd, Pune.

4.3   Job creation

Saoner is in the relatively prosperous State of Maharashtra, but is on the border of Madhya Pradesh, whose population is predominantly made up of so-called tribal people. These are descendants of the indigenous people of India, and they tend to be very poor and marginalized. Millions of these people migrate within India every year in search of the casual labouring jobs on which they have to depend. Particularly large numbers of these people migrate to places such as Saoner which are near to the tribal areas, and Mr Bhalerao realized that the creation of sustainable livelihoods is in itself a valuable social contribution.

The process has therefore deliberately been made as labour intensive as possible. It is possible to mechanize compost production by the use of machinery such as that manufactured by the Excel Company, but Mr Bhalerao wanted to create as many jobs as possible, as well as to limit the amount of capital invested in the business. He built a small warehouse, and he also bought shovels, sieves and baskets for transporting the material, but otherwise everything is done by hand.

The Anamol Krishi Udyog generates more productive employment every year than any other business in Saoner. Fifteen daily wage labourers and one supervisor are employed, full time. They are paid fifty rupees, or about one dollar, for a day's work. This may appear to be a very low wage, but it is well above the rates paid by farmers and other casual employers in the area, and it is regular work. Both men and women are employed and, most unusually, there is no difference in wages for male and female workers.

4.4   Marketing

In spite of the high cost of inorganic fertilizers, and the large quantities that are needed even to maintain crop yields, it is difficult to persuade farmers and other potential users to use compost such as that produced by Mr Bhalerao's business. Inorganic fertilizers show results very quickly, and it is immediately obvious if they are not used. Compost, on the other hand, produces a more long-lasting and sustainable improvement in fertility, but it takes some three or four years for this to take effect. Farmers want instant results, and many cannot afford to wait.

Farmers in the area have been making excessive use of inorganic fertilizers for many years, and this means that rather large quantities of compost are needed in order to restore the soil structure. This makes the local farmers even more reluctant to use compost, in spite of the fact that their crop yields have been gradually falling for several years. The Excel brand of compost is also fairly well known to those people who are familiar with the advantages of compost and use it already; this is of similar quality to the Bhoosampada product, and is sold at a retail price of $100 per tonne.

Mr Bhalerao has used a number of strategies in order to overcome these difficulties. Firstly, he calculated that his production cost was just under $35 a tonne, after allowing for all his costs, so he decided to sell his compost for the very competitive price $40 of a tonne, less than half that of the Excel brand which is the main competitor. Anamol Krishi Udyog's compost is marketed locally, as a local product, within Nagpur and the adjoining districts. It is sold in attractive and convenient 40kg bags, branded with the Bhoosampda name.

About 20 per cent of the total sales were initially made direct to farmers, by agents and by Mr Bhalarao himself, who called on the farmers and personally explained to them the disadvantages of chemical fertilizers and the long-term damage they do to the soil. The remaining 80 per cent of sales were made by agents. They sold the compost through agricultural retailers, and through them to the final users, by distributing pamphlets to the shops, and taking orders from them. Anamol Krishi Udyog also offers free home delivery, cash discounts for prompt payment and a generous commission of 20 per cent to the agents. The compost is also sold to farmers' co-operatives, agricultural universities, government agencies, and plant nurseries.

Thus far, marketing has been a major problem for the business. Mr Bhalerao would like if possible to work in partnership with the bigger companies in the agricultural supplies market. A start has been made with the Ankur Seeds Company. This firm has an extensive and effective marketing network and also has direct contacts with a large number of farmers, and this firm alone appears to have the potential to market almost half the compost produced by Anamol Krishi Udyog.

In spite of the marketing difficulties, the business has been quite successful. During the first year of operations, only 200 tonnes of compost were produced, but four years later, in 2003, production was running at the level of 1000 tonnes per year. This uses just about all the organic waste which is generated in Saoner. The municipality still has to collect and dump the waste, as they had been doing before Mr Bhalerao started his business. Now, however, the organic material is being processed almost as fast as it is dumped. The smell has more or less disappeared, and there is no need for the municipality continually to look for new dumping areas. The dumping site is well maintained, and, as a bonus, Anamol Krishi Udyog pays $100 a year for the use of the waste and the right to occupy part of the site.

4.5   Finance and costs

The investment in equipment and other fixed assets was deliberately very limited, in order to maximize employment opportunities. Nevertheless, the composting process takes several weeks to complete, so that a substantial sum has to be invested in work-in-progress. Sales also tend to be seasonal, since compost is only required around the planting season, so that large amounts have to be kept in stock. The working capital requirement is still further increased by the need to offer some of the more important customers rather generous credit terms.

Mr Bhalarao therefore found that he had to use nearly all his available resources to finance the compost business; he spent the gratuity he had received when he retired from the paper mill, his accumulated provident fund and some of his monthly pension. He also took a loan of nearly $4,000 from the Saoner branch of the Shishak Sahkari Bank.

The approximate cost of producing one tonne of finished compost is shown in Table 4.2.

Table 4.2. Compost production costs

Labourers' wages, twelve person days per tonne of finished compost, at $1.00 per day	$ 12.00
Biological conversion agent, 3kg per tonne of compost, at $2.40 per kg,	$ 7.20
Packaging, twenty-five 40kg bags per tonne of compost, at 20 cents a bag,	$ 5.00
Marketing expenses, including pamphlets and agents' commissions.	$ 6.00
Overheads (includes royalty, bank interest etc)	$ 4.00
Total expenses	**$ 34.20**
Selling price per tonne	$ 40.00
Profit	$ 5.80

The costs of overheads and management, including bank interest, the fee paid to the municipality, travel costs for sales visits, rent of a small office, stationery, accountancy and a nominal stipend of forty dollars a month for Mr Bhalarao himself, are of course relatively fixed, and do not increase in line with sales. The business is thus reasonably profitable after four years; Mr Bhalerao has paid off most of the bank loan, and has also repaid a part of the considerable sum he had to invest in it at the beginning. The working capital requirement has also come down substantially, as large customers such as Ankur Seeds Limited draw their supplies fairly regularly and settle their accounts promptly.

Mr Bhalerao does not believe that he will make a fortune out of Anamol Krishi Udyog, but that was never his intention. He is more than covering the costs of the business, and at the same time he is benefiting his employees, his neighbours, the community environment and his customers; he is more than satisfied.

Note: Indian Rupee amounts have been converted to US dollars at the rate of Rs50 = $1.00

4.6 Conclusions

This case study clearly contains many lessons for any individual or organization that is interested in urban waste composting as a business, and for municipalities or other communities that are searching for ways in which to reduce or eliminate the problems of waste disposal.

Every reader will gain different insights from the example, but the following points seem particularly worthy of mention:

- A small-scale composting business, with a production capacity of 1000 tonnes a year, using the organic waste from a small town, can cover its operating costs and earn a small surplus.

- Urban waste composting may be initiated as a social, a business or a public service venture; a composting business can satisfy a wide range of needs, and the initial motivation is unimportant.

- Related practical experience may be a more important requirement for success than specialized qualifications or sophisticated technical knowledge; the necessary information can fairly easily be obtained, assimilated and applied by someone with general understanding and experience in agro-processing.

- Like any business, urban waste composting involves risks, and success depends on the owners' willingness to make and to learn from mistakes, to improvise and to search for new solutions. Such behaviour is not normally associated with municipal authorities; it is typically entrepreneurial.

- Urban composting is unlikely to be attractive to profit maximizing investors; it is far from glamorous, it has to be undertaken in an unpleasant environment, and the returns may be no more than adequate.

- The process may be highly capital intensive or it may employ quite large numbers of unskilled labour, with negligible investment in fixed assets. Urban composting can create jobs at very low capital cost, and can therefore be a very attractive enterprise in places with high unemployment.

- The process is slow, and sales may be seasonal. The investment in fixed assets can be low, but the working capital requirement may be large, and anyone who undertakes such an enterprise must be prepared for this.

- The initial marketing task may be slow and difficult, because the product and its benefits are unfamiliar. There may also be well-established brands already on the market. Aggressive and ingenious marketing may be necessary; this is not an activity at which municipal authorities are likely to excel.

4.7   Acknowledgements

We would like to acknowledge with thanks the contribution of Mr Amol Bhalerao, who provided the information for this case study.

Chapter 5

Composting in Sri Lanka

Jonathan Rouse

Reviewed by L.C. Jayawardhana

5.1   Methodology used

Fieldwork for this study comprised around one month of field visits to all types of composting plants run by the public and private sectors, NGOs, universities and community groups, as well as a variety of partnerships between these groups. Numerous informal semi-structured interviews were conducted with individual and community composters, employees, managers, planners and funders of composting plants as well as composting buyers. Observation was key, and provided considerable insight into the operations and effectiveness of composting plants as well as the welfare of the composters. In some cases the observed reality was very different from claims made by organizations and literature.

The quality and reliability of data collected in Sri Lanka varied considerably. However, by triangulating between observations, discussions, consultations and literature it was possible to feel confident about certain research findings. Where there is doubt, this is highlighted in the text.

Composting initiatives in Sri Lanka
This section summarizes different types of composting initiatives in Sri Lanka. Information is arranged in tabular form to facilitate comparison between cases.

Box 5.1. Ratnapura Municipal Council

Background

A government-run windrow composting plant, designed to accept around 150tonnes per month (tpm) waste and produce 30tpm compost. The composting site was very poorly planned, and recent consultations regarding improvements have been ignored. It is also poorly managed: the windrows are not turned (leading to bad odours from anaerobic processes), the site is dirty (making a bad impression and associating compost with garbage) and no market had been developed for the compost, resulting in large stockpiling. It was difficult to obtain accurate information from Public Health Inspectors, who knew very little about the project. Observation did not concur with claims made. The plant is based at a large site around 200km east of Colombo

Funding

Donor: Asian Development Bank (ADB) approx US$90,000. Some funding also from World Bank through the Community Environmental Initiatives Fund.

Objective

Solid waste management in response to open dumping of waste.

Key strengths

- Land provided by government.

- Secure source of waste for composting from local authority.

- Provides employment to eight workers. However, salaries very low: lower than other composting plants.

Photograph 5.1. Piles of waste and compost at the Ratnapura site.

Box 5.1 continued ...

Key weaknesses

- Poorly designed site: windrows not covered, so become saturated with rain and produce leachate.

- Low-quality product as mixed waste is used for production.

- Not financially viable and does not produce enough income to pay salaries of workers.

- Fully donor funded, so no one has a stake in success.

- No market for finished compost: this has resulted in production almost ceasing because there is no further storage available for unsold compost.

Box 5.2. Horizon Lanka Private Ltd

Background
A small private company producing and marketing 30tpm 'Habitat', a compost made from agricultural and farm waste. Also helping to run failed composting plants in Sri Lanka and turn them round to be profitable. Office based in Colombo, production in rural areas.

Funding
Private investment.

Objective
Commercial.

Key strengths

- Strong marketing strategy: developed market through awareness raising, education and offering free samples.

- Quality product: no problems with contamination from mixed waste, and compost blended with fertilizers for variety of products.

- Distribution via satellite retail networks.

- Excellent technical expertise, also revenue-making through consultancy services.

Key weaknesses

- Not organically certified: certification prohibitively expensive for small company.

- No export potential for product due to quality and certification problems.

Box 5.3. National Forum of People's Organisation

Background

The National Forum of People's Organisation (NFPO) has set up a small composting project in Madapatha, 10km south of Colombo. Households and market stalls pay workers to collect waste which is taken to a rented piece of land for sorting and composting in windrows. Up to 30tpm of waste is accepted, and the total output of compost is around 6tpm.The project was not running well when visited due to a broken tractor, illness of one of the workers, poor waste collection fee recovery, and difficulty in selling the finished compost.

Funding

Project capital costs were met entirely by the NGO, and ongoing costs are funded partly by sporadic household payments and market collection fee recovery as well as further NGO funds.

Objective

To demonstrate that small-scale windrow composting is possible. It was emphasized that this was designed as a demonstration project.

Key strengths

- If all households paid their waste collection fees and all compost was sold then the project could be economically viable.

Key weaknesses

- At present the project is not economically sustainable as viability relies on revenue from a good collection service which is not in place. The scale of production would also need to increase to enable capital expenses to be covered.

- The quality of compost produced was very poor: it had a high soil content due to rats burrowing under the windrows, and was contaminated due to use of mixed waste stream.

- Very poor market exists for finished compost. The manager said 'There is no time for us to market the product and the existing market is poor and highly seasonal'.

Box 5.4. University of Peradeniya, Kandy

Background

A patented composting unit consisting of a large 10m long chute running down a slope into the top of which part-sorted waste is loaded. The waste gradually decomposes and over a period of about 21 days it works its way down the chute. Compost is harvested at the bottom and is then cured for a further two months before being finally sieved and packaged. The plant can compost around 180tpm of waste, and produces approx 40tpm compost. The composting unit is situated on local authority land provided for free, and is designed and managed by a department of the University of Peradeniya, in Kandy.

Funding

Joint World Bank and private sector funded. Total cost Rs6m (approx $45,000).

Objective

This project is a production-focused large-scale operation. The objective is effective and economically viable management of organic solid waste.

Photograph 5.2. The composting chute in Peradeniya, Kandy.

Box 5.4 continued ...

Key strengths

- This composting plant is paid per tonne to accept waste for composting. It is effectively benefiting from a landfill subsidy.

- Provides employment to 10 people.

- Private-sector interest means there is a focus on making it into a viable business.

- Land has been provided for free by local authorities.

- Good market for compost has been established with a local agricultural fertilizer company who market and distribute product.

Key weaknesses

- Large capital investment is required along with maintenance of complex machines and equipment.

- Contamination levels in compost are too high for certain organic standards.

- Because all types of waste are accepted to the site, occasionally truckloads with a high proportion of clinical or building waste are received.

- The nature of work offered by this plant is considered undesirable, and the plant suffers from high staff turnover.

- The plant is only viable while land is provided free of charge.

- The private investor is mainly interested in construction contracts rather than ongoing operation, as compost production is not profitable enough to be attractive.

Box 5.5. Women's community groups in Galle

Background

Community composting facilitated by 'Artacharya Foundation', an NGO working through organized women's groups. Groups of around five families deposit all their organic waste in a steel barrel. Around 100kg of compost is harvested per month and sold to wealthy local households for around Rs20/kg. Composting is also used in people's vegetable gardens, and this serves as an advertisement as crops have improved. The composting project is operating in Galle, a small town around 200km south of Colombo.

Funding

The main aspects which required funding were initial NGO facilitation and purchase of the barrels. 1200 barrels have been provided to communities free by the NGO, but since the project became 'proven' they are now providing bins via microcredit. The NGO is funded by the Norwegian and Australian governments.

Objective

Poverty alleviation through effective private enterprise.

Key strengths

- Effective community mobilization has taken place.

- The government is supporting the composting activities by using landfill savings to improve infrastructure in composting areas.

- Compost is high quality as it is made from organic waste separated at source. In addition, producers use their own compost which gives an added incentive to make a quality product.

- The market for compost is strong and local. There is no need for transporting to the product. Marketing is by word of mouth.

- There have been many socio-economic benefits; women's groups have strengthened the community:

  'Before these projects we slept lots and fought amongst ourselves. Now the neighbours know each other and are friendly'.

  'Being in groups and doing this has raised our profile and given us access to NGOs and politicians. We are a force to be reckoned with and have bought about change'.

Key weaknesses

- The project may not be easily transferable. For example, it was replicated in Hikaduwa, a nearby town, where it has met with much less success. This is partly because there is a weaker local market but also a stronger household demand for using compost on fields.

5.2   Key issues emerging

Different roles of different groups

It is clear from the cases described that there is a great diversity of expertise, strengths and opportunities among different composting groups. Table 5.1 presents a highly simplified summary of the key strengths and objectives of each composting group.

Table 5.1. Key strengths and objectives of composting groups

Group	Objective	Land	Stake in financial viability	Funds	Willing to take risks	Community skills	Technical expertise	Marketing expertise
Government	SWM	✓		✓				
Private sector	$		✓	✓				✓
NGO	SWM/PR			✓	✓	✓		
University	R&D			(✓)	✓		✓	
Community	SWM/$	(✓)	✓			✓		

Key: SWM - Solid Waste Management$ - Profit
PR - Poverty reduction through employment provision
R&D - Research and Development

During fieldwork various comments were made about groups' comparative advantages or weaknesses, such as the ease with which NGOs can attract donor funding for such things as organic certification of compost (unaffordable to a small business).

It becomes clear that potentially strong partnerships could be established between certain groups with complementary skills. The University of Peradeniya compost chute project is an example of this with its University technical input, government land and subsidy, donor financial support and private-sector interest. Therefore, one of the key points emerging from this analysis is that partnerships are an essential element in ensuring sustainability.

Landfill subsidy

The government, University, NGO and private sector projects all required free land in order to come close to financial viability. An additional form of subsidy was necessary for the others: the waste collection fee for the NGO, and a 'gate fee' for accepting waste at the University. Composting waste saves local authorities considerable sums of money, and those investing in composting are beginning to demand some of the savings. There was talk in Sri Lanka of a landfill subsidy worth 50 to 75 per cent of total savings to local authorities, but this has not yet come into place.

The Norwegian Agency for Development Corporation undertook a study of the Galle community's composting and calculated that each community group saves local authorities around $5,000 per year. As a result of the savings, the women's groups demanded, and secured, some of the money to be invested into their local road and sanitation infrastructure.

Quality issues

Horizon Lanka and the Galle community composters used pure sources of organic waste to make their compost, from farms and kitchens respectively, and as a result they produced high quality uncontaminated compost. By contrast, the other producers faced problems from contamination because their compost was derived from organic matter mixed with domestic, industrial and even clinical waste. Mixed waste can never be satisfactorily separated without the risk of heavy metals leaching into organic matter, and small particles of metal, glass and plastic etc. becoming mixed with the final product. This has serious implications if compost projects are going to be undertaken as a solution to municipal waste problems: source separation is essential.

The other quality issues related to organic certification. The market for organic compost is large and growing in Sri Lanka, which is becoming a major producer and exporter of organically grown foodstuffs. However, organic standards for compost are high, as is the price of organic certification. In addition, standards differ from country to country, so in some circumstances a compost producer may have to pay for a number of tests and certificates. These prohibitive costs make penetrating the organic market very difficult indeed.

Marketing

Horizon Lanka, the University and community projects have succeeded in securing good markets for compost. They succeeded for different reasons:

- Horizon invested heavily in a skilled marketing team which worked over many years to build the market

- The University has come to an arrangement with an agricultural company which buys all a compost then handles marketing and transport itself

- Communities have found a local market and generated demand through word of mouth and building a reputation through demonstration projects.

By contrast, the government and NGO projects have failed to establish markets for their product, and as a result have become so overwhelmed with the compost that they have had to largely stop production. The government had not considered marketing, and the NGO simply did not have the capacity to invest in marketing activities.

Financial viability

The private sector, University and community-run composting activities achieved financial sustainability, albeit with subsidies in some instances. The least financially viable composting project was that of the NGO. While the objective of the project was to demonstrate composting in a peri-urban area rather than to turn profit, NGO projects rarely genuinely turn a profit. In addition, the value of purely technical demonstrations (unless using or developing new methods or technologies) is questionable. It is the application of composting technologies which usually poses the real problems, and financial viability (accounting for any subsidies) which determines their sustainability.

The government project, if better managed, may have been financially viable mainly because it effectively benefits from 100 per cent of landfill savings: the local authorities are simply saving themselves money.

Individual stakes (i.e. investment) in success is also important. As a representative of one NGO in Sri Lanka said,

'NGOs are not geared up to running businesses. A business requires an individual with a personal stake in the success or failure. External funding means we have no personal stake in projects'.

However, it is important to be realistic about the profitability of composting. When one investor in Sri Lanka was asked 'Is composting really an attractive business venture for you?', he replied:

'In terms of business I would drop it tomorrow: a large investment and very slow repayments over 15 years. I would get a better rate of return on my money if I left it in the bank. However, I feel I have some social responsibility having gained a lot through successful business, and I'm keen to see my children inherit a clean Sri Lanka, not one with marshlands full of our dumped rubbish.'

This is telling, and echoes the sentiments of numerous others in Sri Lanka and across South Asia.

Reporting

There is a need for much more accurate, and honest, reporting of successes and failures in composting. Due to pressures of funding, certain actors are inclined to describe abject failures as glowing successes by focusing on single achievements, or simply misrepresenting facts. It is impossible to learn from past experiences until a culture of acceptance of problems and failure is developed.

5.3   Lessons and recommendations

- *Building teams*: recognize and embrace the synergy between different actors in composting, and form partnerships between actors with complimentary skills.

- *Subsidy*: governments need to be convinced of the economic benefits of composting, and begin to pass some of these benefits on to producers.

- *Quality*: source-separated organic waste is far preferable to using contaminated mixed waste for composting.

- *Organic certification*: there is a need to develop standardized, internationally agreed standards for 'organic quality' compost, and to find ways of making a more affordable certification.

- *Marketing*: it is important not just to focus on production, but also to consider how the compost will be sold in the future. Learn from the experiences of others, and appreciate that this is a resource-intensive activity.

- *Financial viability*: ultimately this underpins the sustainability of composting activities. Groups without business skills may consider forming strategic partnerships with those who do.

- *Reporting*: report strengths, weaknesses and problems honestly and openly to enable cross-learning.

5.4   Acknowledgements

LC Jayawardhana was co-researcher for the Sri Lanka fieldwork. She translated, advised and provided invaluable insight during fieldwork and reviewed Chapter 5 of this book.

Chapter 6

Composting in Dhaka, Bangladesh

Jonathan Rouse

6.1 Waste Concern

Waste Concern was founded as an NGO by A.H.Md. Maqsood Sinha and Iftekhar Enayetullah in 1995. It is an NGO which works in close partnership with government, the private sector and local communities to improve solid waste management in Dhaka. It has over 20 members now, and has attracted international funding from organizations including UNDP and USAID.

Waste Concern aims to:

- Improve the environment by promoting waste recycling activities in the country

- Conduct research and experiments on solid waste management, recycling, clinical and hazardous waste management, wastewater treatment and organic farming

- Develop a community/private sector/municipal partnership for improvement of the urban environment, and

- Create job opportunity by promoting recycling of waste[2].

Figure 6.1 illustrates the organizational structure and activities of Waste Concern and its composting plants.

---

2. Text adapted from website: www.wasteconcern.org

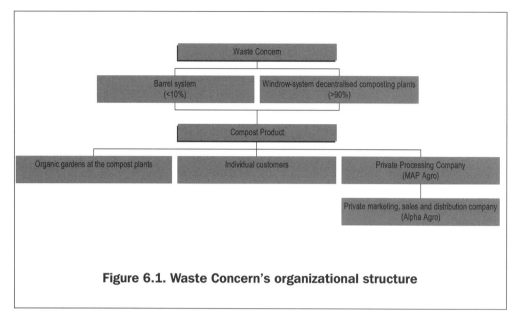

Figure 6.1. Waste Concern's organizational structure

6.2   Windrow composting plants

Waste Concern has established a number of composting plants in Dhaka, but this study focuses on the largest and longest-established: the Mirpur plant. The Mirpur composting plant has been running for eight years and is now operating at full capacity, processing around 3 tonnes of raw waste per day. The plant began as a small experiment, but now provides employment to more than 20 people. Land was donated by the Lions Club and funds for establishing the plant were sought from local philanthropists. Further funds have since been procured from a number of regional and international donors.

The Mirpur composting plant sits on a plot of around 1000 square metres (a quarter acre) in a residential area. There is a variety of housing around the plant, ranging from medium/high-income housing down to informal. Seven men and boys are employed by the plant to collect waste in tricycle-vans from middle/ high-income households around the composting plant. The collected waste is brought to the composting plant where it is sorted. The organic portion is arranged in windrows for composting. Some of the remaining waste (e.g. aluminium, paper, plastics) is sold for recycling by the workers. The rest of the waste is left for collection by the Dhaka City Corporation, who transport it in a truck to the disposal site. Fifteen individuals are employed as production workers. They sort the waste, turn the windrows, sieve the finished compost and weigh and pack it into sacks.

One Supervisor and one Community Worker are also employed at the compost plant. The Supervisor oversees activities at the site and keeps the books and accounts, while the Community Worker is responsible for community liaison, and helped get local residents behind the idea of a paid door-to-door waste collection, as well as a local composting plant.

Benefits to the urban poor

The workforce consists of 2 men, 14 women and 6 boys, all from the surrounding low-income areas. Around half the workforce has been working in the plant for at least three years, indicating a low turnover of staff.

All workers said they prefer this work over previous or alternative forms of employment for a number of reasons, including:

- There is greater flexibility (particularly for bringing infants to work) than in other jobs such as the garments factories where they could not keep their children.

- The management is very reasonable, in contrast to the experience of management in the garments industry where some women were not even allowed to use a toilet frequently, and were beaten.

- Working hours are good, unlike maid or garments work where night-time or evening work results in travelling at night and makes looking after a family difficult.

- The working environment is fairly safe, unlike brick-crushing which can damage the hands.

- Getting a job here does not require a bribe, unlike sweeper jobs for Dhaka City Corporation.

Despite the above, the work was not viewed as very prestigious and a number of the workers lied to their friends about where they worked; they describe the composting plant as an 'office' or 'fertilizer factory'. However, some workers said they were respected for their work at the plant because it was a 'large organization' which is 'doing a public service in cleaning the environment'.

Land for composting in Dhaka

Aerobic windrow composting is very land-intensive, and at present there are no cheap alternatives to this process which make more efficient use of land. Land in Dhaka is very expensive due to scarcity and high demand. Composting does not turn sufficient profits to cover land rental or purchase costs, so composting projects tend to rely on goodwill (i.e. donations of land) or government land leases.

Procuring land for composting in Dhaka can be a challenge for a number of other reasons:

- Residents are often reluctant to have a composting plant situated near their home

- There is a chronic shortage of land in Dhaka, one of the most densely populated cities in the world. Other land-uses may take priority.

The land for the Mirpur plant was donated by the Lions Club, but Waste Concern has also been through the process of acquiring local authority land on lease for composting. An application for a leased plot of land for another composting plant in Dhaka took over two years to process, as it moved from desk to desk within Dhaka City Corporation (DCC). This is not only a symptom of administrative weaknesses, but also of a lack of clear policy on composting within the organization. It may also reflect the low priority given to composting. The reason land was eventually granted to Waste Concern for the other composting plants was because of the cost-savings the DCC would realize in terms of landfill reduction.

Waste Concern is a respected, high-profile and not-for-profit organization that has good relationships with local authorities and politicians. Despite this, the organization faced many difficulties in obtaining land for composting in Dhaka. Given this, it seems likely that a private investor or small community group would find it almost impossible to procure local authority land on lease, and may not be able to afford the time to invest in the application. It may be that, in time, DCC will develop a policy on this which will make land more easily available to NGOs as well as community and private investors.

6.3　Barrel composting plants

Waste Concern has also initiated a number of small 'barrel' type composting projects in low-income areas in Dhaka. Individual or small groups of families are provided with a concrete or steel barrel measuring around 120cm high by 70cm diameter (see Photograph 6.1). Organic waste is placed into the barrel and harvested as mature compost from the bottom after a period of around four months. The compost is sold to Waste Concern for Tk2 per kg (about US$0.04/kg).

Photograph 6.1. Waste Concern barrel composting

Benefits to the urban poor

Composting barrels have resulted in a number of positive outcomes for the poor, including:

- An extra source of income. Amounts earned varied considerably, but according to research ranged from between Tk20 to 100 per family per month. This is significant against wages of little over Tk1000 per month.

- Cleaner streets and local environment because organic waste is no longer dumped openly.

- Increased awareness of waste issues, and better handling of other waste.

- Health benefits resulting from cleaner local environment. Evidence for this is only anecdotal from slum dwellers: for example, one man stated that there was less diarrhoea since composting barrels had been introduced.

- Improved relations with wealthy neighbours, because the local environment is being kept cleaner.

- Improved relationships within and between slum families because of collaboration.

In some slums the barrels have been very popular, but their introduction has not been without problems.

Cost

Waste Concern is providing barrels free to users in the projects in Dhaka. The cost of a metal barrel is Tk2300 (approximately US$45) including installation. At Tk2 per kg for compost, each barrel would have to produce over 1 tonne to pay for itself. This is likely to take over a year at reported production rates. Although this repayment period is reasonable, the initial cost is still a barrier to many poor families in slums. Tk2300 is equivalent to the cost of a cycle rickshaw, and is more than most families could afford without credit. Therefore either credit facilities or some kind of subsidy would be required if barrels were not being provided free of charge.

Even if this sum was available to families on credit, individuals may choose to spend the money on more profitable livelihood investments which are less risky and quicker to recoup.

Investing in informal settlements

The threat of sudden eviction from slums combined with the possibility that metal barrels will be stolen and the fact that they corrode tends to discourage people from investing in barrels. Building regulations for informal settlements dictate that no permanent structures may be erected, and a brick-built barrel might constitute such a structure.

Location

'Not in my backyard' (NIMBY) attitudes have prevailed in some slums, particularly where alleyways are narrow and/or people do not like the thought of a 'dustbin' near their home. The compost bins can also look unsightly and drip leachate. At times they will also smell bad and although odours can be controlled by sprinkling sawdust periodically, the barrels are reported to attract flies. Vermin are also attracted by recently deposited foodstuffs.

Where space is very limited, a compost bin may have to compete with more profitable use of space such as a cigarette stall, a working area (e.g. for a tailor) or extra living quarters. Space is always an issue in Dhaka.

Politics and participation

While in some slums barrel composting has been undertaken enthusiastically and families have accepted the concept, in others it has been less successful. Families in one slum, inhabited by Dhaka City Corporation sweepers, were reluctant to use the barrels partly because they did not wish to start separating their waste, but partly because of political issues in the slum. These issues were related to who controls the slum, and the threat to their jobs they perceived from the composting activities. This resulted in composting barrels being sabotaged and having human faeces dumped in them, rendering them useless.

6.4   The market

There appears to be a high level of awareness of the need for organic material for agricultural land, and a number of individuals consulted in the research knew about the composting process, either from childhoods spent in villages or from the television. However, compost from waste is not always the preferred choice for farmers who may choose to use freely available cow-dung or who doubt the quality and safety of products derived from garbage.

The largest potential market for compost is organic farmers who require continuous supplies for their land. Many farmers are keen to switch to organic farming methods because of the premium prices organically grown produce can fetch, as well as problems they encounter from using chemicals on their land. Problems include health issues from chemicals, and spiralling costs as the quality of their land deteriorates and requires ever more chemical inputs year by year.

During the first year a farmer switches to organic farming, a very large quantity of compost is required to get to the soil 'into shape'. According to two NGOs in Dhaka , this first year can prove more expensive than buying chemical fertilizers for the year. Despite savings on each subsequent year when less compost would be required, as well as long-term improvements (rather than deterioration) of land, this first year can prove too great a barrier for many farmers. It is a major disincentive to the adoption of organic practices in Bangladesh.

A further market issue relates to quality. It is important that the quality of compost is consistently high and pure. One of the advantages of Waste Concern selling their finished compost to MAP Agro is that MAP have machinery for grinding and cleaning the compost. Their machines reduce any shards of glass to harmless powder, catch pieces of metal and remove polythene using an air-sorter. This process is obviously time-consuming, but farmers consider it important so it is a necessary investment.

Heavy metal contamination is another issue for farmers, and it is the difficulty in being able to control these that makes organic certification difficult if using compost derived from domestic waste. According to tests on samples of Waste Concern's compost, contamination levels were found to be lower than those allowed in India. Of course, the raw materials for compost made from domestic waste may vary considerably day-to-day, so it is dangerous to draw too much comfort from one test result, and there may always be dangerous aberrations.

6.5 Marketing and private-sector partnership

Waste Concern produces many tonnes of compost each week. Staff appreciate the importance of marketing in order to shift their product and generate profits. The market for Waste Concern's compost falls into two main categories:

- Low-volume sales to individuals. These are often middle-class householders purchasing compost for their gardens. Selling price: Tk10/kg

- High-volume sales to MAP Agro, a private chemical fertilizer processing company. Selling price: Tk2/kg

MAP Agro buys around 300 tonnes of compost from the NGO every month. They blend some of it with chemical fertilizers, and sell it to MAP Agro, an agricultural input distribution company.

Although Waste Concern stands to make more clear profit from sales to householders, there are various advantages to selling low-price/high-volume to established agricultural companies. These include:

- Once the business relationship with the distribution company is established, no further marketing is required by Waste Concern. Map Agro are confident that they could sell up to ten times the present volume of compost purchased from Waste Concern. This is indicative of the scale of the market for compost as well as the effectiveness of this arrangement. Using a well-established agricultural input company also lends credibility to compost as an agricultural product, as it sits alongside 'modern' chemical fertilizers, positively perceived by many farmers.

- No transport, distribution or sales infrastructure is required by Waste Concern (e.g. lorries, regional sales points etc.). Alpha Agro, another company used by MAP Agro, distributes the compost up to 620km from Dhaka, using existing transport and sales infrastructure.

These factors leave Waste Concern to pursue what it is good at: composting. In Bangladesh this is proving to be a successful model which other NGOs elsewhere may be wise to follow.

6.6   Other issues for composting in Dhaka

A number of key composting issues have been raised with specific reference to Waste Concern. This section describes a number of other areas which relate more generally to composting activities in Dhaka.

Location

In deciding upon the location of a compost plant in Dhaka, a number of conflicting issues needed to be considered and balanced by Waste Concern:

- Most domestic waste is generated in cities, but the main market for compost lies in rural areas.

- Land prices in Dhaka are very high compared with rural areas

Transportation costs in Bangladesh are high. Raw waste reduces to as little as 20 per cent of the original volume and mass when composted, and it is more hygienic to handle and transport compost than waste. Given these factors, it is wise to produce compost near to the source of waste (as in this case in Dhaka), leaving transportation for the finished product.

It is interesting to note that the situation for Waste Concern in Dhaka is very different from the situation in a smaller town such as Khulna, where waste is generated much closer to the market for compost. In such situations cheaper land might be procured on the outskirts of the town, still necessitating minimal transportation of waste, and locating the composting plant close to the market.

Viability

A detailed study of the financial viability of the Mirpur compost plant has been undertaken by Isabelle Rytz (2001)[3]. This shows that the plant is now a viable activity. Costs were said to have been covered at the plant after 23 months. The study accounts for costs such as buildings, vehicles and personnel etc. as well as some other important (but less obvious) costs such as bribes to DCC truck drivers for non-organic waste removal. Although this expense is 'informal' it is important to include this in developing a picture of true viability. Waste collection fees from householders can be seen to make an important contribution to the overall profitability of the plant.

---

3. Assessment of decentralised composting scheme in Dhaka, Bangladesh: Technical, operational, organisational and financial aspects, SANDEC/EAWAG, Switzerland, and Waste Concern, Bangladesh, Rytz, I., 2001

Two areas in this economic analysis need to be highlighted. Firstly, the issue of land. Land prices are not included in this economic analysis. This is justifiable for the case of Waste Concern which is in fact not paying anything, and has never paid anything, for the land it is using. Given that the private sector or community groups may not be able to take advantage of rent-free land for composting, it is important to recognize this omission. Because profit margins are relatively low, if full rental value of land had to be met, this composting plant would no longer be viable.

The second area relates to the hard work of NGO staff in sensitizing and liaising with local residents. Community sensitization plays a key role in determining levels of participation in community collection and composting schemes which in turn, as described before, contributes significantly to the overall viability of compost. This has been undertaken very effectively by Waste Concern. Although it is a time and skill-intensive process, personnel costs do not appear on the economic analysis. If a business were to establish a composting plant it is unlikely they would have community development skills, and so would have to buy in skills. In the case of some of Waste Concern's composting plants, they would have to be employed specifically on sensitization and liaison for up to one year: a considerable expense and, again, not on the balance sheet.

6.7   Key lessons learned

*   The social and political capital of the organization running a composting plant plays a significant role in the land acquisition and affects the running and sustainability of the activities. In the case of Waste Concern, they are a respected organization with good relations with local authorities and this enables them to acquire land in the city.

*   At present, one of the constraining factors of aerobic windrow composting is the space it requires. For high-priced urban land it is not a competitive commercial activity. There is a need for the development of less land intensive composting technologies. Waste Concern is presently testing 'effective micro-organism' solutions which are designed to speed the process of composting, and thus reduce the land demand.

*   The model of linking with the private sector for distribution and marketing of compost appears to be very successful in Bangladesh. Although this lowers the final selling price for the producer because it introduces a middleman, it enables the producer to concentrate on production.

- Waste Concern also has an important role in training and extension work because it is a high-profile organization with the skills and capacity for this. Although a business may not engage in these activities, it is important to have 'champion organizations' in countries to set examples, and experiment, document and advocate.

6.8   Acknowledgements

Thanks to A. H. Md. Magsood Sinha and Iftekhar Enayetullah of Waste Concern for co-operation and assistance during research in Bangladesh.

Uthpal Palash acted as co-fieldworker and translator in Dhaka.

Chapter 7

Waste busters, Lahore, Pakistan

Anjum Pervez

Waste Busters, Karachi

7.1   Introduction

Lahore is a city with a population of 7 million people, generating about 3500 tonnes of solid waste every day. The Solid Waste Management Department (SWM Dept) of the City Government of Lahore is responsible for the collection and disposal of this waste. The city is divided into six towns comprised of union councils. Each town is responsible for its waste management services but all report to the Central Waste Department of the Lahore City Government. Waste Busters launched its community waste management project under the banner of 'Lahore Sanitation Program' in 1996. It is called community waste management because the community is mobilized through local community-based organizations and community workers who motivate the community to put their waste in garbage bags for door-to-door collection and to make regular payments. The programme has been replicated in other major cities of Pakistan.

The main components of the Waste Busters programme were community participation, door-to-door collection, segregation of inorganic from organic wastes and composting.

7.2   Waste collection

Waste Busters has devised various mechanisms to collect the waste from member households and other places in Lahore. The project started with an initial membership of 1000 households in 1996 and by June 2002 the number of houses getting the service in Lahore was 10,000. Public campaigns for awareness of proper waste management techniques and the need for community participation are carried out jointly with the city government. The primary source of waste for the project is the daily door-to-door collection in garbage bags through its own collection staff to the 10,000 households in its membership. The membership charge is banded according to the income level of the locality. This ranges from high-income areas with a charge of Rs100[4]/month and middle-income areas with Rs50/month to low-income areas where the charges are Rs30/month. In high-income areas, the service includes provision of garbage bags, daily pick-up in vans and street cleaning, with a 100:1 ratio of households to workers. In middle-income areas, the services are performed on donkey carts. Garbage bags are not provided and waste is collected every day. Households keep their waste in used shopping bags. The ratio of labour for street cleaning is 200 households per labourer. In the low-income communities, the service is performed by handcarts and waste is lifted on alternate days. No bags are provided to the households. Of the total number of households served about 60 per cent of membership is in the high-income areas, 20 per cent in middle income and 20 per cent in low-income areas. The waste is finally transported to the transfer station and rejects are disposed of.

The second source of wastes is the clippings from trees and grass etc. from home gardens. The wastes generated at the fruit and vegetable markets are also a rich source of organic material for the composting process. In addition to these organic wastes, animal wastes such as cow dung, poultry waste, rice husk and sugar cane mud are also used for composting purposes. In total, approximately 100 tonnes of waste is collected by Waste Busters every day. In some cases, Waste Busters pay for the waste at the following rates:

Cow dung   Rs500/tonne

Poultry waste   Rs1200/tonne

Rice husk   Rs500/tonne

Sugarcane mud   Rs750/tonne

In addition to the wastes collected by their own vehicles, Waste Busters also get help from the local municipal corporation, which arranges for dump trucks in case of heavy loads during storms etc.

The typical composition of the municipal waste collected is given as follows. Sampling is done at the point of disposal from the garbage truck to the sorting plant. For the average of 100 tonnes of waste collected, the breakdown is:

---

4. Rs 50 = 1 US $ in 2002

Item	Percentage	Tonnes/day
Organic	55%	55
Plastics	20%	20
Paper	5%	5
Glass	3%	3
Metals	2%	2
Rags	5%	5
Tetrapak	3%	3
Debris	7%	6

7.3   The waste recycling and composting plant

The project gradually developed a programme to recycle the organic wastes into compost, which was presented in the market as 'Green Force'. Recycling of the waste was always the ultimate target of the project as the final disposal of waste has always been problematic: the municipality has insufficient land for a proper landfill site and the collection fees cover only the cost of collection. Composting of the organic wastes was considered appropriate in order to become self-sustainable and to generate income, as 60% of the total waste generated in Lahore is organic. The main streams of organic waste are kitchen waste, garden waste, fruit and vegetable market waste and cow dung. There are no existing formal-sector uses for municipal solid waste except occasional landfilling.

Waste pickers in Lahore picked out most of the readily saleable items from the inorganic waste stream even before our waste collection teams reached the households. Therefore the income from inorganic recyclable items was very low. Since there was no commercial level composting plant operating in the entire country at the time, it was considered as a viable alternative to the common practise of using the raw manure.

The recycling element of the project was initiated in 1998 and culminated in a full scale composting plant by the year 2000, processing 100 tonnes/day of solid waste. Although source separation was tried so as to minimize the labour on sorting after collection, the experiment failed. Households did not bother to segregate or put different wastes in the designated bins and all of it was mixed even when separate bins were provided. Further public education, combined with financial and social incentives, is still required. Additional waste has been brought from the Parks and Horticulture Authorities for disposal. Waste from fruit and vegetable markets was also brought for composting. The proportion of municipal solid waste was 50 per cent, garden waste 30 per cent and the market waste 20 per cent by weight.

Currently the project employs 50 people including Mechanical Engineers, a Soil Scientist, Laboratory Technicians and skilled labour. Daily input of mixed waste is 100 tonnes per day. This produces 30 tonnes of compost per day.

The demand for compost is year round, however peak seasons are for rice and wheat when the demand and sale of compost goes up by 50 per cent. The demand comes from a range of users, such as commercial farmers, landowners, landscapers, home gardeners and vegetable growers.

Finance

The cost for the 100 tonnes/day recycling plant was Rs10 million (US$175,000) in plant and machinery. The land used is about 4 hectares about 10 per cent of which is used for the machinery and the rest is occupied by windrows. This land was provided free. The monthly operating costs are Rs500,000 including salaries, utilities, maintenance etc. The sales are at the rate of about Rs1500/ tonne and average at about 500 tonnes/month (tpm). In the non-peak season the production is reduced to 10 tonnes/day, or 300tpm.

The capital financing for the project was arranged entirely through private resources. The banks and other financial institutions were not willing to finance projects related with waste recycling as the concept was new at that stage. There is certainly a good demand for the compost and since there is not much competition at the moment it seems to hold a bright future.

Segregation process

The entire waste collected is passed through a waste segregation process which includes mechanical as well as manual sorting of inorganic waste from the total waste collected. The mechanical segregation involves a hopper from where the entire waste passes through a screening tunnel. The tunnel segregates the wastes according to size. Waste smaller than 10cm drops through a chute to a sorting conveyor and the rest goes to the main sorting conveyor which is 21 metres in length. Workers then pick out the plastic bags, paper, rags, glass, etc. from the conveyor belt and put them through chutes into storage bins. The organic waste is left on the conveyor and goes through to a cutter which shreds it into 7cm pieces before it is transported to the windrows area. The inorganic waste is packed in bales and sold for recycling to glass, paper and plastic industries. The rejected waste is collected and put into an incinerator for burning. The energy from this process is used for drying and so on.

Composting

The organic waste remaining is then transferred to the composting area where the windrow composting method is used to process it into organic fertilizer. The windrow method was adopted after trying various options, because it is the most cost-effective and quick solution for the decomposition of organic wastes. Windrow composting consists of placing the mixture of raw materials in long narrow piles or windrows, which are agitated or turned on a regular basis. The equipment used for turning determines the size, shape, and spacing of windrows. Bucket loaders with a long reach can build high windrows; turning machines produce low, wide windrows. Waste Busters uses bucket loaders.

The organic waste is then spread in the shape of a windrow, 3 metres wide, 21 metres long and 1.5 metre high. Layers of cow dung and poultry waste are used to augment the organic matter. The windrows are sprayed through a sprinkler system with water which carries micro-organisms specially induced through molasses. Aeration of the windrow is important to expedite the decomposition of the organic wastes and to activate the micro-organisms induced in the organic matter. These micro-organisms play a very active role in early processing of the wastes and composting is completed within six to eight weeks rather than the normal six to eight months. These micro-organisms are available at the rate of Rs30/litre.

Windrows are aerated primarily by natural or passive air movement (convection and gaseous diffusion). The rate of air exchange depends on the porosity of the windrow. If the windrow is too large, anaerobic zones occur near its centre, and these release odours when the windrow is turned. On the other hand, small windrows lose heat and may not achieve temperatures high enough to evaporate moisture and kill pathogens and weed seeds.

Turning mixes the materials, rebuilds the porosity of the windrow and releases trapped heat, water vapour and gases. Although the pile is aerated by turning, the new oxygen within the pore spaces is quickly depleted by the micro-organisms. The most important effect of turning is rebuilding the windrow porosity. Turning 'fluffs up' the windrow and restores the pore spaces eliminated by decomposition and settling. This improves passive air exchange.

7.4   Marketing

Developing a range of products

Many people are well aware of the benefits of using organic matter in their soils. Most compost is used in the spring and early summer. It is therefore important that the compost produced is stable and suitably dry for delivery at that time. The compost must meet the needs of the target market. For example, many commercial nurseries need compost primarily for its soil building qualities and not necessarily for its nutrients. On the other hand, organic farmers prefer compost products with high nutrient concentrations. Many home gardeners want compost that is uniform, clean and free of contaminants. Offering a variety of compost increased sales and developed a larger market.

One of the first marketing questions to consider is how to sell compost - in bulk, in bags or in both. Bags accommodate customers who need compost in small quantities and are conveniently handled at retail outlets. Bagged products also sell at approximately three times the price of than most bulk compost. The higher price justifies higher transportation costs and therefore a larger market area. The prices quoted previously exclude transportation cost, which could be Rs20 per kilometre per truck. Sometimes, demand comes from a remote location. Waste Busters has been transporting compost up to 1000km, but that makes the product very expensive. Ideally sales should be limited to a 200km radius.

Bagging clearly expands the potential market, but the bagged compost market is served by large-scale commercial composting only because of the costs of equipment and labour for bagging, and storage of the bagged product during the off-season. Quality control is also more critical since the compost may remain in plastic bags for a relatively long time.

For small volume requirements, Waste Busters offers bagged compost locally as a soil improver for home gardens. Some customers also come and bring their own tractor trolleys and buy in bulk at their own transportation cost. Small packets of 1kg and 5kg are now sold in retail stores, plant nurseries and department stores. Small local level advertising campaigns are arranged to publicize the availability of the product at these stores.

Although the bulk market is more favourable, the transportation costs keep those sales very local. A larger market has therefore been developed with wholesale nurseries, landscapers, public and private housing projects, municipalities, new home builders, greenhouse operators and organic gardeners where the common packing is in 50kg polypropylene bags.

In addition to compost, Waste Busters provides a composted mulch material and topsoil amendment grade, a nutrient-rich fertilizer grade and a potting media grade. The other products, powder from compost and compost in pellet forms are sold in packets of 1kg and 5kg at the nurseries and 50kg for farms. The powder has levels of nitrogen-phosphorus-potassium (N.P.K.) of 5-3-2 and a maximum particle size of 1mm. It sells for Rs150 per 50kg bag.

Although the characteristics that users require of compost vary with the specific use, compost users generally share several common expectations. These are listed below, roughly in order of importance.

Quality

Good quality compost is probably the number one requirement from the user's standpoint. A user's judgement of quality depends on the ultimate use, but common criteria include moisture; odour; feel; particle size; stability, nutrient concentration; and a lack of weed seeds, phytotoxic compounds and other contaminants. The product must also be consistent, it must have nearly the same moisture content, particle size and/or nutrient concentration from batch to batch. If not, customers never gain confidence in using it. A consistently stable product is particularly important; just one bad lot of compost will turn away customers forever if it harms their plants.

Users assess the compost by the quality of their produce, texture of soil and the physical appearance, and these indicators are also used by the manufacturers as benchmarks. A quality control facility has been established in the plant with laboratory assistance to check the nutrient values, percentage of organic matter and pH level. A laboratory analysis is made for each batch of compost that is produced and it is checked for heavy metals. The laboratory manager issues a clearance certificate before the product is allowed for sale. The marketing department then ensures proper packing, labelling and shipment to the respective dealers. One example of the packaging is 50 kg polypropylene bags with a clear inscription of the trade mark: 'Green Force' Organic Soil Conditioner. It clearly states the ingredients and the nutrient (N.P.K.) values of the compost.

Price of product

The price must be competitive with other organic compost substitutes, e.g. cow dung, poultry waste, top soil, peat moss and so on, though a higher price can be offset by high quality and performance. The price differential between the compost being marketed and cow dung is about Rs500/tonne which the customer is willing to pay due to the benefits of using compost compared with cow dung.

Information

Although farmers are aware of the fact that using organic matter in the soil is a good thing, most potential customers are unfamiliar with compost's characteristics. At least initially, they want and need information about its benefits and how to use it. For some users, the most important information is an analysis of the N.P.K. nutrient concentration and pH level. Many users also desire information about application rates and application procedures.

Target markets and demand

Over the years, Waste Busters has developed a niche in three target markets. The biggest market for the compost is high value crop growers such as vegetable and fruit farmers, horticulturists, flower growers and landscapers, as it is considered more environment friendly than raw cow dung or other manure. A second market that has developed is the landowners with problem soils such as saline soils where they use the compost to improve the soil. The third market is the home gardens where the compost is sold through nurseries etc. in small packets. Farmers make up 50 per cent of the market, problem soils 20 per cent and home gardens 30 per cent. Waste Busters is the only producer of properly composted organic matter in the market. The price ranges from Rs1500/tonne in bulk to Rs15/kg in small packets for home gardens.

As people see the effects on the soil, the demand for compost is growing day by day. Although it is only possible to estimate, the anticipated future demand for compost can be said to be over one million tonnes a year based on the current market trend. This is a conservative target based on minimal input of 0.5 tonne per acre on 3 per cent of the total cultivated land in Pakistan, which according to the Food and Agriculture Organisation's survey is approximately 22 million hectares.

7.5   Sales and promotion

The marketing of the compost is being done through various methods. The most common marketing tool has been the provision of free compost for experimental and demonstration plots. Where this is done in a small area with comparative plots in adjacent farms, results are recorded in plant growth, soil condition and actual yields. The results are used by the field marketing staff as examples to promote sales.

Samples, leaflets, information brochures, newsletters, website and newspaper advertisements are also used to promote the product.

Typical users of the compost are farmers and growers who are aware of the benefits of a soil conditioner. They buy compost to enhance their soil structure and make it more productive. Emphasizing the positive benefits of compost is normally sufficient to convince a prospective buyer of its value. The fact that compost is made from recycled products is also helpful. Although customers may gain satisfaction from participating in a recycling effort, the compost is offered as a valuable resource, not as a treated waste material.

Distribution

A distribution network is established throughout the country with a distributor in each District. The distributor is basically a stockist who has storage capacity and then sells to dealers within his district who are appointed at the Tehsil (small group of villages) level. The dealers then have agents at village level. There is also a margin from the distributor to the agency holder which is divided among them through mutual agreement. Major fertilizer companies have not shown any real interest in co-operation with these sales efforts, although they have been approached. The dealers network is supported in its marketing by a nationwide media campaign by Waste Busters. Seminars, farmer meetings and exhibitions are arranged to promote the concept of organic farming and use of compost.

7.6   Conclusions

Composting has certainly taken a major role as a solution to the waste management problem in the cities in Pakistan. As many as five major cities have made plans to install composting plants to deal with organic wastes that are being produced in large quantities all over the country. There are no such strategies at the government level so far, although awareness about organic matter is now becoming more and more common. The Ministry of Environment as well as local governments support compost programmes.

This experience is a prime example of a private-public partnership where the city government has provided land and infrastructure for the establishment of a compost plant, the corporate sponsor has financed the plant and machinery and Waste Busters is responsible for the waste collection, sorting, recycling and marketing of the compost from this plant. The project has been successfully launched and is now in full swing, providing bulk compost to the surrounding areas.

There are no real constraints in promotion of compost; however, there is a need to promote the concept of organic farming by the agriculture department which it is not yet taking this up as an issue.

This as a project has been documented by various agencies so that it can be replicated in other cities. Another compost plant has been established and production started in January 2002 in the city of Jhelum to replicate the compost plant in Lahore. A multinational corporate sponsor transferred the design. Learning from the successful experience in Jhelum and Lahore, Waste Busters has now been approached by the city governments in Gujrat, Multan, Islamabad and Karachi to replicate the system in the respective cities. The model that has evolved from the experiences so far is that the local government should provide the land and transport waste, the private sector should finance the projects on a loan basis, and civil society should make the project run successfully by involving the local communities.

Part 3: Guidelines for Composters

Chapter 8

Key findings

Most of the projects described in the case studies were initiated by non-governmental organizations or individuals as a means of promoting compost as a business for the urban poor. The projects are located in different cities of South Asia and although they all operate in different contexts they share a number of common issues.

8.1 Ensure a reliable waste collection

One of the reasons that compost projects are initiated is to contribute to a reduction in the quantities of waste requiring final disposal. Composting is a way of reducing the quantities of organic (putrescible) waste. Projects studied reveal improved environmental conditions in residential areas. Waste no longer overflows at communal bins, thereby reducing the amount to be collected by the municipality. However, one of the important elements in improving the local environment through composting is a reliable solid waste collection system. Compost projects without a proper primary collection system may not sustain the public's co-operation.

8.2 Encourage local authorities to offer support

Urban waste composting may be initiated as a business or a social or public service venture. A composting business can satisfy a wide range of needs, and the initial motivation is unimportant.

Common challenges for all composting projects were identified as constraints to replication on a city-wide level, and a common difficulty is the lack of municipal acceptance and support. Municipal support for decentralized schemes was observed to be limited to the provision of land only. In some cases sites are usually allocated in an informal manner and so the composting schemes do not have any legal backing. However, local authorities could play a significant role in supporting the compost projects by assisting with training, community education, collection of unrecyclable waste and buy-back arrangements. They may also arrange proper disposal of reject waste.

8.3   Develop less land-intensive techniques

At present, one of the constraining factors of aerobic windrow composting is the space it requires. For high-priced urban land it is not a competitive commercial activity. There is a need for the development of less land-intensive composting technologies. Some NGOs, such as Waste Concern, Bangladesh, are testing 'effective micro-organism' solutions which are designed to speed the process of composting, and thus reduce the land demand. Further field testing of approaches which require less land is necessary in order to sustain and replicate the composting projects.

8.4   Establish good relations with local authorities

The social and political capital of the organization running a composting plant plays a significant role in the land acquisition and affects the running and sustainability of the activities. Large NGOs are respected organizations with good relations with local authorities and this enables them to acquire land in the city. This may not the case for smaller organizations.

8.5   Develop business plan, market research and strategy

Development of adequate strategies and the identification of market segments for compost are some of the prerequisites for successful and long-term operation of decentralized composting. Most of the projects examined lack an appropriate business plan or a marketing strategy. A timely assessment of different improvement options is required, such as direct marketing or the use of already available outlets through other contractors. The initial marketing task may be slow and difficult, because the product and its benefits are unfamiliar. There may also be well-established brands already on the market. Aggressive and ingenious marketing may be necessary; this is not an activity at which municipal authorities are likely to excel.

8.6   Do not expect large profits

Composting activities do not readily generate financial profits. The process is slow, and sales may be seasonal. The investment in fixed assets can be low, while the working capital requirement may be large, and anyone who undertakes such an enterprise must be prepared for this. However, a fairly small-scale composting business with a production capacity of one thousand tonnes a year, using the organic waste from a small town, can usually cover its operating costs and earn a small surplus. Urban composting is unlikely to be attractive to profit-maximizing investors: it is far from glamorous, it has to be undertaken in an unpleasant environment, and the returns may be no more than adequate.

8.7 Unskilled labour can be employed in place of machinery to create jobs

With the use of machinery to produce large quantities of waste, the composting process may be highly capital intensive or it may employ quite large numbers of unskilled labour, with negligible investment in fixed assets. Urban composting can create jobs at very low capital cost, and can therefore be a very attractive enterprise in places with high unemployment.

8.8 Governments should pass on economic benefits

The benefits of composting are environmental and economic. Governments need to convince everyone of the economic benefits of composting, and begin to pass on some of these benefits to producers.

8.9 Collect input-output information

The data collected during the field study revealed a scarcity of documentation on mass flows and unclear financial figures. Numerous cases lack an information database and project planning is therefore not possible. Input-Output Tables for waste, compost and recyclables as well as monthly Cost-Revenue Balances would increase transparency and would also provide a sound basis for negotiations with the municipal authorities. Improved data documentation would thus increase the professional status of citizens' initiatives as well as junior companies. Organizations need to report strengths, weaknesses and problems honestly and openly to enable cross-learning.

8.10 Training and extension work

Waste Concern has an important role in training and extension work because it is a high-profile organization with the skills and capacity for this. Although a business would be less likely to engage with these activities, it is important to have 'champion organizations' in countries to set examples, and experiment, document and advocate.

8.11 Partnerships

There are some good examples of partnerships. In one case local government provides the land and basic infrastructure such as access roads, electricity, water etc. and the NGO arranges for the plant and machinery. The NGO operates the plant and 15 per cent is paid to the local government as its share for the contribution in infrastructure. This experience is a prime example of a private-public partnership where the city government has provided land and infrastructure for the establishment of a compost plant, the corporate sponsor has financed the plant and machinery and the NGO is responsible for the waste collection, sorting, recycling and marketing of the compost from this plant.

Chapter 9

Marketing compost

Jonathan Rouse, Claire Richardson and Mansoor Ali

Marketing is an extremely important part of any sustainable composting project. This chapter introduces some of the principles behind understanding demand and stimulating a market for compost. It focuses on compost derived from urban organic waste in low-income countries, but from a marketing perspective as opposed to a solid waste or environmental perspective. It is written as a simple guide to the marketing of compost for readers with no prior background in marketing. It will be of value to those running compost plants at present who wish to understand their market better, as well as for anyone proposing to establish a compost business who needs to understand the market. This chapter is based on the assumption that it is desirable (and possible) for all compost producers to sell their product. As such, from this point on, all compost producers are referred to as 'businesses'.

The users of compost are a diverse group, consisting primarily of farmers (especially organic), nurseries and home-gardeners growing both flowers and vegetables. Compost is also commonly used by local authorities for landfill cover and landscaping in parks and municipal spaces.

9.1   What is marketing and why do composters need it?

Marketing can be described as the business of moving goods from the producer to the consumer, i.e. selling products. The marketing perspective holds that the purpose of a business is to create and keep customers and guide businesses towards producing desirable products at the right price.

Marketing is concerned with the process of exchange of a service or product, usually for money. It provides tools enabling businesses to face the challenge of creating and keeping customers and accelerates the process of exchange. Marketing is concerned with two main areas:

1. The marketing environment: this includes external forces such as legislation, environment, technology and competition etc. Much of the marketing environment is difficult to control for a business, but it is possible to exploit opportunities and be aware of threats.

2. The product and its market: this involves understanding your market (i.e. customers) and matching your product and the way it is promoted to your market's needs, and/or targeting your product at a certain market.

One of the main problems faced by composters is in finding, stimulating or establishing a market for compost, and lack of market is one of the main reasons for the bankruptcy of composting plants. Compost is a bulky product and cannot be endlessly stored. Compost producers need marketing:

- Composters can benefit from selling compost to increase revenues from their operations, as well as solve storage problems.

- Composters wishing to provide employment opportunities in viable composting plants require a sustainable market to generate income.

- Composters rely on increasing sales of compost to expand business.

The key: customer satisfaction

Customer satisfaction is central to marketing. Farmers and gardeners can choose where they buy compost, so a business continually aims to satisfy its customers through improved products and deliveries. If it fails to satisfy customers, the business loses the customers. In order for a business to be able to satisfy its customers, it must first understand them.

Market research and analysis

Market research is about finding out who customers are, what they need and want from compost and how to provide them with the right product at a price they are both willing and able to pay. There are a number of steps involved in understanding and analysing your market as follows.

- Understanding the marketing environment

- Understanding your market

- Using the Marketing Mix

The following sections explore these steps in more detail.

9.2   Understanding the marketing environment

Often composting businesses operate within a highly complex and dynamic environment, which is impossible to control and often difficult to predict. It is, however, important for a business to have a good understanding of the environment in which it operates, as the environment can present a multitude of opportunities and threats to a business. The external factors and forces may be:

- political
- legal
- regulatory/policy
- societal/cultural
- 'green'/environmental
- economic
- competitive
- technological.

It is essential to analyse the environment on a continual basis and keep up to date with changes that affect your business directly and indirectly, now and into the future. It is also worth noting that in the marketing environment opportunities can become threats and threats can become opportunities.

Opportunities and threats analysis

An opportunities and threats analysis is an aid to understanding the marketing environment. It involves taking each environmental factor by turn and considering the direct and indirect opportunities and threats they pose. Opportunities and threats can then be considered and/or ranked according to:

- the significance of their potential effect
- their imminence
- the degree to which it is possible to react, either to maximize benefits from an opportunity or minimize the effects of a threat.

Table 9.1. Marketing environment analysis - opportunities and threats

	Opportunities		Threats	
Factor/force	Direct	Indirect	Direct	Indirect
Political forces				
Legal forces				
Regulatory forces/policy				
Societal/green forces				
Economic forces				
Competitive forces				
Technological forces				

Competition

Businesses must always consider their competitors, as they are a potential threat to success. Competitors are the other businesses who offer customers compost or a product that performs, or is perceived to perform, a similar task, such as manure and fertilizers.

The following are examples of questions your business should be asking to understand the nature and strength of competition. More specific issues relating to competition are discussed later in the chapter.

- Consider what business and product types pose a threat to your business (e.g. other composters, fertilizer companies, cow dung etc.)

- Undertake a survey of these, and gather information about them.
  - e.g. size, investment, history, nature/area of market

- Find out in which market 'segments' the competition is strongest.
  - Should you target your product elsewhere, or can you compete?

- Find out what future competition may look like, e.g. are lots of businesses taking up composting?

- What advantages do the competitors have over your business? e.g. more funds for investment, a better transport network.

- How do your business's capacity and resources compare to those of competitors? What are the implications of this, if any?

- What do the competitors do better than your business? Do you need to change something?

- What disadvantages do these businesses have compared with yours, e.g. Not as good a reputation in the market. Can you capitalize on this?

- What lessons can you learn from your competitors?

- How is your composting businesses competing with its competitors? Is it on product, price, place or promotion? Do you need to respond to a weak area or capitalize on a strong one?

9.3   Understanding your market

Market analysis is the gathering and analysis of information about your market, i.e. customers.

Want, need, and ability and willingness to pay.

Customers of use to your business must have a need or a want (or both) for your product, as well as an ability and willingness to pay for it. Table 9.2 illustrate this principle. The last column indicates whether each individual scenario comprises

Table 9.2. Understanding your market

Scenario	Need	Want	$$$ Able	$$$ Willing	Market?
1. A rural farmer needs compost for his fields which have very poor soil. He realizes this, and wants to buy some. However, although he thinks the price is reasonable, he is simply unable to pay for the product as he is too poor.	✓	✓	x	✓	x
2. A wealthy householder uses compost for growing flowers on his balcony. He wants compost but does not have a great need for it (his plants would grow without it, and he could afford chemical fertilizers).	x	✓	✓	✓	✓
3. A nursery owner needs compost for healthy plant growth, and wants to buy quantities monthly. He is a successful businessman and would be able to pay the price, but considers it too expensive, so is unwilling, despite the impact on his yields.	✓	✓	✓	x	x
4. A tea grower does not want compost but has been advised that his soils are degrading and he needs to add soil conditioner. He is able and willing to buy compost.	✓	x	✓	✓	✓
5. The Government wishes to see an expansion in organic farming and subsidizes compost and provides loans to farmers.	x	✓	✓	✓	✓

a potential market for compost. Note that not all components need to be present; for example, in Scenarios 2 and 4, need and want are not simultaneously present, but they still comprise viable markets. In Scenario 1, as in 5, the market is only there if it is possible to secure the required finance

Segmenting the market

The next step in understanding your market is to segment it. This involves sub-dividing the compost market into different customer groups each with similar characteristics and requirements. The market could be segmented by, for example:

- Occupation (e.g. farmers, nurseries)

- Geographical locations (e.g. rural, urban)

- Purchasing power/ability to pay (e.g. wealthy householders versus poor rural farmers)

- Crop type (e.g. food, non-food - with implications on quality)

- Frequency of compost purchase etc. (e.g. farmers once per year

- Scale of demand (e.g. farmers large demand, home growers small demand).

Broadly we can deal with these segments in two groups: the present market and the potential market.

The present market

The present market comprises those who are buying or willing to buy compost at present. If compost is not supplied directly, middle-men may be the customers and analysis will be applied to them.

 Activity 1:Draw up a table describing your present market segments, as in the example shown.

Remember to consider customers who have previously bought compost from your composting business and one-off sales. Are these glimpses of larger untapped markets?

The potential market

The market of today is not necessarily going to be the market of the future. Although it is impossible to predict the future it is important to consider what new customers may exist in the future.

Table 9.3. The present market by segment

Segment	Description	Volume	Frequency	Comments (including where, income, reliability etc.)
Farmers	Rural agriculture	High	Seasonal/annual demand	Considerable distances - transport implications. Low ability to pay, reliable demand.
Nurseries	Mostly urban or peri-urban flower or plant growers	Medium	Seasonal	Often a local market. Medium ability to pay, reliable market but considerable competition including from home-made compost
Middle/high-income households	Private gardeners using compost for vegetables or flowers	Low	Not strongly seasonal, though peaks during spring	Local market, high ability to pay and repeat custom/ distribution simple

The potential market comprises those who are buying compost from a competitor, and those who want or need compost but do not know about it or are not convinced.

 Activity 2:Draw up another table similar to that for the present market, and complete for potential market segments. Consider:

- Possible future/new uses for compost (e.g. parks, landscaping) and who you would need to pursue to realize these markets.

- The present level of awareness in each potential market segment for compost (i.e. what proportion of customers in each market segment know about compost?)

 Activity 3:Collect information on ability and willingness to pay for each of the market segments. Also consider reasons which may assist you in addressing low willingness to pay.

Market demand

Now that we understand the structure of the present and potential markets, we need to try to quantify demand.

Demand is measured in terms of monetary value per year. It is important to understand the present and potential demand for compost in the market as a whole as well as in each market segment. The two examples in Box 9.1 illustrate calculations of present and potential demand for two hypothetical market segments.

Box 9.1. Calculating market demand

1. Present demand
- How many farmers are buying compost?
- How much compost is purchased per year?
- What is the value of the compost purchased?

[Total present market for specified segment] =
[Number of customers] x [tonnage purchased per year] x [tonnage price]

This indicates the market value of this market segment in $/year.

2. Potential market demand
- How many farms are in this area?
- How much land do these farms cover?
- How much compost is required per acre?
- How much compost would be purchased if farmers were to begin using it?
- How often would compost be purchased?
- How much compost can farmers afford?
- Estimate the price to be charged

[Total potential market for specified segment] =
either: [Number of customers] x [tonnage purchased per year] x [tonnage price]
or: [Total acres] x [tonnage required per acre per year] x [tonnage price]

When demand has been calculated for each of the present and potential market segments, they can be added together to give totals for demand.

Other important considerations include:

- Are the market segments expanding or contracting? (i.e. Are more or fewer customers, in each market segment, buying compost?)

- Is demand for compost seasonal or steady in each market segment?

- What has been the past pattern of customers buying compost? (i.e. How often do customers purchase compost in each segment and how much?)

- What determines whether or not customers purchase compost? (i.e. Is it education, being aware of the compost, the quality of compost etc?)

Targeting market segments

You have now segmented your market, quantified the value of each segment and considered some other important factors such as whether it is expanding or contracting, seasonality, reliability, and what the future holds for present and potential markets. Armed with this information, it will be clear that your business /location/product is more suited to certain market segments than others. It is very often advantageous for a business to target marketing towards a particular market segment or selection of segments. Your product may be exactly what one segment needs, but not meet the needs of another. You should choose your target markets according to how well your business can perform compared to competition.

9.4   Using the 'Marketing Mix'

The Marketing Mix, also known as the 'Four Ps Framework', is integral to ensuring successful marketing. The four Ps are:

- Product: A quality product that satisfies customers' wants and needs

- Price: The price must be right in the eyes of the customer, as well as generate revenue

- Place: Where the business is in relation to the market, and how to reach it

- Promotion: Raising awareness and understanding and promoting your product to customers

The challenge for a composting business is to get all four Ps right from the viewpoint of their customers to enable sales and repeat sales. They all implicitly concern product, market and competition. A business must find out what customers need and want from their compost, where and how they can best get the compost to the customer. It must also understand the price that the customers are happy with and can afford to pay, and the best way of letting their customers know about the compost, its benefits, and how and where to buy it. Finally, in order for a business to succeed it must do all of this at least as well as, if not better than, its competitors.

The following sections guide the reader through the four Ps. However, they are not isolated concepts, and there is considerable overlap and interconnection between them.

9.5   Product

The first element of the marketing mix is product. This section looks at how to ensure sales and repeat sales.

It is important to carefully consult customers: they are the key to your business and hold the answers to much of what you need to know about your product and how it needs to be marketed. The following questions provide examples of the kind of information you need to gather.

Each of the following can be applied to the individual market segments.

- What is compost used for?
- What do people want from compost? Does your product offer/promise/deliver this?
- What is the customers' perception of the use of compost?
- Why is compost being bought from your business?
    - How much and how often does the customer buy your compost?
    - Seasonal variation?
- Is the market limited by customers, cost or supply of compost? (i.e. do people buy as much as is available, or just as much as they can afford?)
    - If it is limited by supply, how much would the customer like to buy?
- Are your customers generally satisfied or dissatisfied with the compost?
    - What does the customer think of the quality of the compost?
    - What do customers not like about your compost? (e.g. high heavy metal content, glass fragments, price etc.)
    - What improvements would your customers like to see in your product?
- Packaging:
    - What does the customer think of the packaging of the compost?
    - Does the packaging affect the customers' choice of compost?

- Are there any particular reasons for the customer wishing to buy compost from your business? (e.g. it is environmentally friendly/helped the poor in production).

- Can customers contact your organization to enquire or complain about the compost? How?

Competition

Your product needs a competitive edge, be that in price, quality, ease of procurement or reputation. You need to understand how your product compares to that of your competitors in the eyes of your market.

- Find out about your competitors' products

  - How does your compost compare to the competition? Which has the competitive edge?

- Do your customers also buy compost from your competitors? If so, why? If not, why not, and can you capitalize on this reason?

Production

The following questions relate to the production of compost.

- What volume of compost can be produced per day/week/month?

- Does this meet the customers' demand for compost or do customers have to wait?

- Describe the standards by which the compost is being measured, e.g. national composting standards, agricultural standards, or self-imposed standards

  - If standards apply, does your compost comply with these standards?

  - What measures need to be undertaken to ensure the quality of the compost?

  - Can you explain any variation in the quality of compost that your business is producing.

- Could the compost be improved?

- The production process:

  - What are its efficiencies/inefficiencies? What can be done about these?

  - What can go wrong in the production process? How are these/can these be controlled?

- How is the quality of compost being monitored? How could it be monitored?

Box 9.2. Developing an array of products

Waste Busters in Pakistan have developed a range of products suited to different segments of their market. They say:
'Offering a variety of compost increased our sales and developed a larger target market. In addition to compost, we also provide a:
- composted mulch material,
- topsoil amendment,
- nutrient-rich fertilizer-grade compost, and
- potting media.'

See Chapter 7

9.6   Price

The price of compost is critical for three main reasons:

- You need to generate revenue and profit

- You need to compete with other producers and products

- The price must be right in the eyes of the customer.

Revenue and profit

The price needs to be right from a costs and profit perspective. For a self-sustaining business this is ultimately the most important factor: if it fails to cover all costs and raise profit for future investment the business will eventually collapse. In simple terms, from a business perspective, price can be calculated as follows:

Price = Cost of production (labour and raw materials) **+ Profit**
(to cover any fixed costs and provide a reasonable profit for future investment)

Some questions to consider:

- What price are you charging or planning to charge, and why?

- Are you covering all of your outstanding costs with compost sales?

- Are there other sources of revenue, such as a household collection fee?

- How much compost needs to be sold at what price to ensure that all costs are covered, and profit made for maintenance and capital depreciation?

For a local authority plant, which does not necessarily depend on full cost recovery or profit in order to keep going, price can be based more on customer willingness to pay.

Customers and competition

Customers want quality products at low prices. Ideally, your product will be cheaper than competitors' and at least as good quality. However, consumers are interested in more than just price.

- If your product is the same price or more expensive then it must have a competitive edge to sell, e.g. higher nutrient level, better quality control and purity etc.

- Note that factors such as reputation can sell products at high prices. Consider designer clothes which are often disproportionately more expensive than they are better quality than standard clothes. There is, however, a strong market.

- Quality of service, or promoting the product as 'green', or one that has provided employment for the urban poor can also convince potential customers to buy one product over another.

It is vital that you speak to your customers and bring together what you have found out about your product with customers' attitudes and willingness or ability to pay. You may find that wealthy customers are willing to pay a higher price for compost if they know it has provided employment opportunities for the poor. A poor farmer, however, may be prepared only to pay a low price as that is all he or she can afford.

The following questions provide further guidance on product price-setting:

- Are customers happy paying your business's present price for the compost?

  - Why/why not?

- How easily are customers able to pay the present price of the compost?

- Are the customers able to purchase as much compost as they want at this price?

- Elasticity of demand:
    - If the price was higher, would customers stop buying compost?
    - If the price was lower would customers buy more compost?
- Are customers mostly satisfied or dissatisfied with the price?
- Do customers buy your compost because of the price?

It is also important to consider your competition. What alternatives exist (e.g. manure, cow dung, fertilizers), and how much do they cost? Do customers purchase cheaper compost from competitors, or would they if the competitors' product was cheaper? Consider putting in place a price/competition monitoring system, as competition is a dynamic factor.

9.7   Place

This section considers the location of your business and market, and how your product reaches your market.

Location

Location is important because you need to optimize your position in relation to your market, staff, supply of raw materials, cost of land, and other considerations specific to your context.

 Activity 4: Buy or make a map. It is useful to get a visual idea of where your business is in relation to supply of raw materials, labour, transport networks and your market.

- Mark on your map the locations of the production unit, raw material and customers.
- Use different colours for market segments.
- Consider the circumstances for each market segment.
- Compare costs and benefits of different locations.

Distribution

Distribution is concerned with transport used (anything from people and wheelbarrows to long distance trucks and trains), routes taken, and the people involved in the stages of distribution (e.g. middlemen or dealers).

Compost produced from the municipal waste is often marketed through distributors because of the low quantities required by individual customers. It is worth mapping the distribution process of your composting business. It does not have to be exact: improvise where necessary. Here is an example.

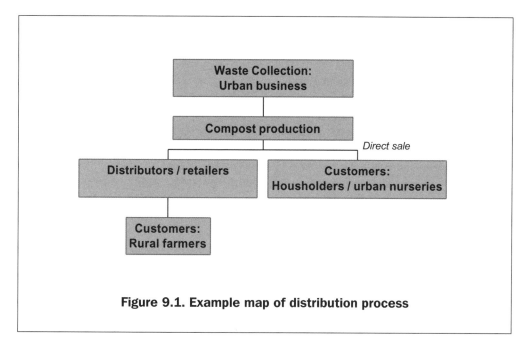

Figure 9.1. Example map of distribution process

The following questions provide a guide to some of the issues to explore relating to location and distribution.

- What direct and indirect routes are you using to reach your customers?

  - Consider the market segment by segment - these could be very different.

  - Who is involved in the distribution process at different stages?

  - Carefully consider all intermediaries. Are they merchants (who sell the compost under their own name) or middlemen (who simply pass on the product at some profit)?

  - What do customers feel about the intermediaries? Should you be looking to increase/reduce their role?

- Does the end consumer know the source of the compost?

  - Are there any advantages of the customer knowing the source of the compost? This may affect your promotional activities.

- Is the distribution process efficient (e.g. cost/time/labour)?

  - Is distribution taking place in the best way possible?

  - What alternative distribution channels exist?

- Consider which distribution channels are the most profitable, and which is most convenient for the customer.

- Does the distribution network used make your compost more or less competitive (e.g. caters for isolated or small-scale customers)?

Box 9.3. Example of compost distribution in Bangladesh

Waste Concern, an NGO in Bangladesh, is producing 300 tonnes of compost per year in central Dhaka. The market, however, is mostly based in rural areas far from Dhaka. The NGO overcame transport problems by linking with a fertilizer company called Alpha Industries, which has established national distribution networks, and so is better placed to reach distant rural markets. Waste Concern is still able to make money from compost sales, and does not have to develop capacity for distribution itself (See Chapter 6).

Competition

Consider your competitors in terms of location and distribution channels.

- Where are competitors based and where is their market?

- What advantages and disadvantages do they have over your business?

- How do your competitors distribute their product?

  - What can you learn from this? Could they distribute yours? Could you combine/complement each other somehow?

- What market segments can they not reach? Could you?

9.8   Promotion

The purpose of promotion is to stimulate demand, and is particularly useful for turning 'ability to pay' into 'willingness - or even keenness - to pay'. Promotion is useful for:

- Telling your customers about the benefits of using compost,

- Informing customers about improvements made to the compost,

- Building awareness in the market about your compost, and

- Encouraging customers to buy your compost as opposed to from your competitors

In the same way as there is a marketing mix, there is a promotions mix - better known as the communications mix, (outlined in Table 9.4). Some or all elements of this array can be used at any one time, according to needs, the message you are trying to communicate, the audience (potential customers) and, of course, cost.

Table 9.4. The communications mix

Word of mouth	Where one customer tells another about your compost
Selling techniques	Face-to-face selling to the customer
Advertising	Communication via print, television, radio, billboard etc
Sales promotion	Encouraging people to buy more. e.g. 'More for less', cheap trial periods etc.
Direct marketing	Door-to-door sales, mailouts, telephone calls
Publicity	Good publicity is always important and includes any published material about your business i.e. press releases
Sponsorship	Where cash from one business supports an activity (e.g. sport) usually in return for advertising and association with popular activities
Exhibitions	Displays promoting and demonstrating products
Identity	Developing a logo or catchphrase, for example, as well as an image which encourages people to feel confident and comfortable in dealing with you as a company
Packaging	An important way of attracting first-time customers as well as getting marketing information across to customers (e.g. product is environmentally friendly or provided employment for urban poor)

Word of mouth, where one customer promotes a product to another, is often the most important method of communicating with your customers. If your product is unsatisfactory, however, word of mouth can also be powerful in worsening the reputation of your product and business. 'It is said that a satisfied customer will only tell one person about a product, but that a dissatisfied customer will tell ten'.

Consider the following questions:

- When and how has your business used promotion in the past?
  - List the messages that have been promoted in the past or at present.
  - List the reasons why these messages have been important.
  - What promotional tools have been used to communicate with customers?
- What are the successes and failures of past experience?
  - Use examples from competitors or similar organizations to your own.
- Think about what your customer really wants. Ask them!
  - What type of promotion works and what doesn't under different circumstances?
  - What helps to promote compost? e.g. environmentally friendly, organic?
  - Find out how your customers found out about your compost.
  - Find out what communications channels would be best to use to reach them.
- What funds are available for promotion? How much would different forms of promotion cost, and what is the possible scale of return?
  - If no funds are available, how can free promotion be achieved?
- How do your competitors promote their compost?
- Which compost are customers most aware of? Yours or competitors'? Why?
- Promotion can change the reputation of a product or company. What do you need to work on to improve the reputation of your company over another?

9.9   Concluding words

By now you should know about:

- The opportunities and threats your business faces
- Your competition
- Your market segments, characteristics and trends, and
- Your business in terms of product, price, place and promotion.

Box 9.4. Promoting your product according to preferences in Lahore

Waste Busters in Pakistan are promoting their product to farmers, and are aware of what works best, and of what their market does and does not want. Their most powerful promotion tool is demonstration, where a plot of land is used to show the difference between plant growth where compost is used. They also write:
'Farmers buy compost to enhance their soil structure and to make it more productive and receptive. Compost is not in vogue because of its environmental benefits; simply because of its physical advantages. Although some customers may gain satisfaction from participating in a recycling effort, we promote compost as a valuable resource not as a recycling project output.' (See Chapter 7)

This information needs to be assimilated and provides the springboard for developing a marketing strategy for your company. Based on marketing information, you can develop a product which meets the needs and desires of your most promising market segment(s) at the right price. You will also be able to carefully plan your promotion and sales methods.

9.10 References

Almeda, R. 2002. Interview conducted in Colombo, Sri Lanka. Unpublished.

De Silva, R. 2002. Interview conducted in Kandy, Sri Lanka. Unpublished.

Pervez, A. (2002). Personal Communication. Waste Busters, Pakistan.

Bibliography

Useful publications

ACTION AID India (1996) A *manual on composting techniques*. ACTION AID: Bangalore.

Ahmed, Rehan (2001) *Compost and its utilisation*. Association for Protection of Environment (APE) / WASTE: Karachi, Pakistan

Alberta Environment (1999) *Leaf and yard waste composting manual- Revised edition*, Alberta Environment, Olds College: Edmonton, Canada.

Alberta Environment (1999) *Mid-scale composting manual*: Alberta Environment, Olds College: Edmonton, Canada.

Alders, C., et. al., (1994). "Wastes wanted." ILEIA Newsletter - for low and external input and sustainable agriculture vol 10(3): 4-5.

Allison, M, Harris, P.J.C, Hofny-Collins, A.H & Stevens, W (1998) *A review of use of urban waste in peri-urban interface production systems* DFID project R6446 (with diskette).The Henry Doubleday Research Association (HDRA): Coventry, UK

Ambrose, J. (1982). Recycling in Developing Countries. Recycling in Developing Countries. Kozmiensky. *Some principles of composting and some science behind composting*

Asomani-Boateng, R. (1993). Planning for domestic solid waste in developing countries: a pilot project of community composting in Accra, Ghana. Regional Planning and Resource Development. Waterloo, University of Waterloo.

Asomani-Boateng, R & Haight, M (1999) *Assessing performance of mechanised centralised composting plants in West Africa: The case of Teshie Nungua composting plant in Accra, Ghana.* Article. Warmer Bulletin No.69: Residua Ltd: UK.

Asomani-Boateng, R., Haight, M. (1999). Reusing organic solid waste in urban farming in African cities : A challenge for urban planners. Urban Agriculture in West Africa - Contributing to Food Security and Urban Sanitation. O. B. Smith, IDRC: 138-154.

Asomani-Boateng, R., Haight, M., Furedy, C. (1996). "Community composting in West Africa." Biocycle 37(1): 70-72.

Avery, I, (2000) *Composting.* Article. Municipal Engineer Volume ME139 Issue3. Institute of Civil Engineering (ICE): UK

Baker, A (1997) *Waste management in Mali.* Article. Warmer Bulletin No. 57. Residua Ltd: UK

Barker, A.V. (2001) *Evaluation of composts for growth of grass sod.* Article. Department of Plant and Soil Sciences, University of Massachusetts, USA: Communications in Soil Science and Plant Analysis.

Benka-Coker, Marian O, & Bafor, Benson E (1999) *Waste management and water pollution (Nigeria).* Paper presented at the 25th WEDC Conference, Addis Ababa, Ethiopia: WEDC, Loughborough University: Loughborough, UK.

Bhattacharyya, P, Pal, R, Chakraborty, A & Chakrabartik (2001) *Microbial biomass and activity in laterite soil amended with municipal solid waste compost.* Article. Department of Geology and Geophysics, Indian Institute of Technology, West Bengal, India: Journal of Agronomy and Crop Science.

Bhamidimarri Rao, S. M., Pandey, S. P. (1995). Aerobic Thermophilic Composting of Piggery Solid Wastes. 3rd International Conference on Appropriate Waste Management Technologies for Developing Countries, Nagpur, India.

Bhawalkar, U. S. (1994). "Converting wastes into resources." ILEIA Newsletter - for low and external input and sustainable agriculture vol 10(3): 20-21.

Bhawalkar, V., Bhawalkar U. (1991). Vermiculture Biotechnology, Frontrankers.

Biey, E. M., Mortier, H., Verstraete, W. (2000). "Nitrogen transfer from grey municipal solid waste to high quality compost." Bioresource Technology(73): 47-52.

Bijlani, H.U, Pande, R.P & Jain, R.C (1974) *A semi-mechanised compost plant for Delhi*. Delhi, India

Biocycle (1989). "The Biocycle Guide to Yard Waste Composting." Biocycle, Journal of Waste Recycling.

Biocycle (1999). The Composters' Answers Book - Solutions from experienced professionals on composting operations. Biocycle, Journal of Composting and Recycling. Emmaus, Pennsylvania, The JG Press Inc.

Brewer, L. J., Sullivan, D. M. (2001). "A quick look at quick compost stability test." Biocycle(1): 53-55.

Brinton, W. F. (2001). "An International Look at Compost Standards." Biocycle(4): 74 -76.

Brinton, W. F., Evans, E. (2001). "How Compost Maturity Affects Container Grown Plants." Biocycle(1): 56-60.

Bio-waste management, USA Ltd (1993) *Business plan April 1993*. Bio-waste management, USA Ltd: Dover, Delaware

Block, D (1998) *Managing the business side of composting operations*. Journal article. Biocycle

Bonhotal, Jean, Rollo, Karen (1996) *Compost because rind is a terrible thing to waste*. Cornell wastes management Institute: Cornell university: Ithaca NY

Brandjes, P., van Dongen, P., van der Vee, A. (1989). Green Manuring and Other Forms of Soil Improvement in the Tropics, Agromisa Wageningen The Netherlands.

Bresson, L.M, Koch, C, Bissonnais, Y, Le Barriuso, E & Lecomte, V (2001) *Soil surface stabilization by municipal solid waste compost application*. (Journal article) UMRV Environment et Grandes Cultures, Thiverval-Grignon, France: Soil Science Society of America Journal.

Broder, M.F (1999) *Results of a Microbial Weathering Study of Composted Explosives Contaminated Soil Obtained from the Umatilla Army Depot Activity, Hermiston Oregon, Second Phase Testing (September 1998-September1999)* Report.Tennessee Valley Authority: Muscle Shoals, Alabama

Brook, Robert & Davila, Julio (eds) (2000) *The peri-urban interface: a tale of two cities* University of Wales, Bangor Development Planing unit (DPU), DFID Natural Resources Systems Programme: Hemel Hempstead, Herts

Capital Compost and Waste Reduction Services LLC, Menands, NY (2000) *In-Vessel Organic Waste Composting Project* Report: NYSERDA00-07: New York State Energy Research and Development Authority: Albany, USA

Caribbean conservation Association (CCA) (1993) *The cover up* (25min. video) CCA - Available in the WEDC Resource centre

Central Public Health Engineering Research Institute (CPHERI) Council of Scientific Industrial Research (1974) *Solid waste in India: final report 1971-1973(Prepared under Foreign Research Agreement No.01-504-01)* CPHERI: Nagpur

Centre of Environmental Education Bangalore (undated) *1. Garbage in Bangalore 2. Clean up Kodagu* (21min. video) Centre of Environmental Education Bangalore- Available in the WEDC main resource centre.

Chandler, John (2000) *The waste strategy 2000 for England and Wales*. Article. International Directory of Waste Management (ISWA) Year Book 2000/2001: James and James (Science Publishers) Ltd: London, UK

Churchill, D.B, Horwath, W.R, Elliott, L.F & Bilsland, D.M (1998) *Low-Input On-Farm Composting of Grass Straw Residue*. Agricultural Research Service, Beltsville, MD. Oregon State University, Corvallis. Agricultural Experiment Station.

Ciavatta, C., Govi, M., Pasotti, L., Sequi, P. (1993). "Changes in organic matter during stabilization of compost from municipal solid waste." Bioresource Technology(43): 141-145.

Ciavatta, C., Govi, M., Simoni, A., Sequi, P. (1993). "Changes in organic matter during stabilization of compost from municipal solid waste." Bioresource Technology(43): 147-153.

Cillie, C.G. (1971) *The composting of urban refuse.* WNNR CSIR Technical Guide K19.

National Institute for Water Research, Council for Scientific and Industrial Research (CSIR): National Institute for Water Research: Pretoria, South Africa.

Clark, G.A., Stanley, C.D., & Maynard, D.N. (2000) Municipal solid waste compost (MSWC) as a soil amendment in irrigated vegetable production. (Journal article) Kansas State University, Biological and Agricultural Engineering Department: Transaction of the ASAE.

Coad, A. (1997). Lessons from India in Solid Waste Management, Loughborough Univ. of Technology Loughborough U.K.

Cochran, J. T. (1992). National Composting Program, United States Conference of Mayors: US Solid Waste Composting Facility Profiles, Volume II.

Cointreau, S. J. (1987). Integrated Resource Recovery: Solid Waste Recycling - Case Studies in Developing Countries (Draft), The World Bank Washington INFWU. 59 pp.

Cointreau, S. J., Gunnerson, Ch. G., Huls, J. M., Seldman, N. N. (1985). Integrated Resource Recovery: Recycling from Municipal Refuse: A State-of-the-Art Review and Annotated Bibliography. (UNDP Project Management Report No. 1.), The World Bank Washington + UNDP. 214 pp.

Collacicco, D. (1982). "Economic aspects of composting." Biocycle.

Collet, John (1994) *Composting sanitation studies & applied research paper prepared for the second LASF Workshop, Mexico City, 24-26 November1994 organised by SIDA Action Research Programme on low cost sanitation.* Aga Khan Health Service Northern Areas & Chitral: Pakistan.

Composting Council (1999). An Overview of issues surrounding the evaluation of the use of the canadian standards for heavy metals for fertilizer products by the association of american plant food control officials, Composting Council USA.

Cooper, Jeff (1999) *Waste minimisation and Recycling: Choosing the best practicable options for solid waste management.* Article. International Directory of Solid Waste Management (ISWA) YearBook 1999/2000: James & James (Science Publishers) Ltd, London, UK.

Cornell Waste Management Institute (1998) *Compost: Truth or consequences* (15 min video on home composting including a users guide) Cornell Waste Management Institute: Cornell university: Ithaca, NY

Cornell Waste Management Institute (undated) *compost because rind is a terrible waste* (7min video) Cornell Waste Management Institute: Cornell university, Ithaca, NY

Cornell Waste Management Institute (undated) *compost because rind is a terrible waste* (30-min. video) Cornell Waste Management Institute, Cornell University: Ithaca, NY

Cornell Cooperative Extension (1994). Composting: Wastes to Resources.

Cossu, R., Muntoni, A., Scolletta, A., Sterzi, G. (1995). Utilization of MSW Compost in Landfills: Effects on Leachate and Biogas Quality. 5th International Landfill Symposium, S. Margerita di Pula, Cagliari, Sardinia, Italy, CISA, Environmental Sanitary Engineering Center.

CPIS (1993). Enterprises for the recycling and composting of municipal solid waste; Volume 1, Conceptual Framework. Jakarta, Centre for Policy and Implementation Studies (CPIS) and Harvard Institute for International Development (HIID).

Crecchio, C, Curci, M, Mininni, R, Ricciuti, P &Ruggiero, P (2001) *Reclamation of a burnt forest soil with municipal waste compost macronutrient dynamic and improved vegetation cover recovery.* Article. Dipartimento di Biologia e Chemica Agroforestale ed Ambientale, Universita di Bari, Bari, Italy: Bioresource Technology.

Crowe, M., et al., (2002). Biodegradable municipal waste management in Europe - Part 3. Copenhagen, European Environment Agency: Topic Report. [www.eea.eu.int and http://europa.eu.int

Cuevas, V. C., Cruz, C. E. (1991). Illustrated Manual on Mass Production of Compost Fungus Activator. Manila, Ecology Laboratory, Institute of Biological Sciences, CAS, University of the Philippines at Los Banos UPLB.

Cuevas, V. C. (1997). Rapid Composting Technology in the Philippines: Its Role in Producing Good-Quality Organic Fertlizers. Extension Bulletin 444. Manila, Ecology Laboratory, Institute of Biological Sciences, CAS, University of the Philippines at Los Banos UPLB.

Cuevas, G, Blazquez, R, Martinez, F &Walter, I (2000) *Composted MSW effects on soil properties and native vegetation in a degraded semi-arid shrubland.* Journal article. Department of Sustainable use of Natural Resources, I.N.I.A, Madrid, Spain: Compost Science & Utilisation.

Dalzell, H. W., Biddlestone, A. J., Gray, K. R., Thurairajan, K. (1987). FAO Soils Bulletin: Soil Management: Compost Production and Use in Tropical and Subtropical Environments, Food and Agriculture Organization of the United Nations Rome. 177 pp.

Darzell, H.W. (1979) *Composting in tropical agriculture: review paper series No.2. (2nd print 1981)*: International Institute of Biological Husbandry

Debosz, K., Petersen, S. O., Kure, L. K., Ambus, P. (2002). "Evaluating the effects of sewage sludge and household compost on soil physical, chemical and microbiological properties." Applied Soil Ecology 19: 237-248.

Department of Environmental Health (1975). "Sanitary Effects of Urban Garbage and Night Soil Composting." Chinese Medical Journal 1(16): 407-412.

Deportes I., Benoit-Guyod J.-L.& Zmirou D(1995) *Hazard to man and the environment posed by the use of urban waste compost: a review.* The Science of the Total Environment, 30 November, vol. 172, no. 2, pp. 197-222(26) Elsevier Science

De Twaalf Ambachten (The Twelve Trades). (1993) *Guide to building your own compact composter (CC).* De Twaalf Ambachten: Boxtel, Netherlands.

Dewar, G.A.(1999) *Waste management in Spain- new horizon.* Article. Warmer BulletinNo.64: Residua Ltd, UK.

DHV Environment & Infrastructure- The Netherlands, Plancentre-Finland & University of Soil Management-Austria (1998) *Composting: A European survey*. Article. Warmer Bulletin No. 58: Residua Ltd, UK.

Diaz, L, Savage, G & Golueke C (1999) *Sustainable Community Systems: The role of integrated solid waste management*. Article. Warmer Bulletin: Residua Ltd, UK.

Diaz, L.F., Savage, G.M., Eggerth, L.L. & Golueke, C.G. (1996). *Solid waste management for economically developing countries*. Cal Recovery Inc., International Solid Waste Association (ISWA): Denmark

Diaz, L.F., Savage, G.M., Eggerth, L.L, Golueke, C.G.(1993) *Composting and recycling municipal solid waste*. Lewis Publishers: Florida, USA.

Dickson, N., Richard, T., Kozlowski, R. (1991). Composting to reduce the waste stream. New York, Northeast Regional Agricultural Engineering Service.

Diener, R.G., Collins, A, Meneses, R, Morris, M & Dame, A (1996) *Political implications for integrating composting into solid waste management in West Virginia, USA*. (The science of composting: part 1) Blackie Academic & Professional: Glasgow, UK

Dixit, Radha Charan (1989) *The feasibility studies on the disposal of solid wastes of Delhi City by incineration: a project report for the degree of Master of Engineering (Environment)* Delhi college of Engineering: Delhi, India

Dorau, D. A. (1992). Solid Waste Compost Standards. 85th Annual meeting & Exhibition, Kansas City, Missouri, June 21-26.

Dow AgroSciences (2001). Clopyralid and Compost, Dow AgroSciences,.

Drechsel, P., Quansah, C., Penning de Vries, F. (1999). Urban and peri-urban agriculture in West Africa - Characteristics, challenges and need for action. Urban Agriculture in West Africa - Contributing to Food Security and Urban Sanitation. O. B. Smith, IDRC: 19-40.

Dulac, Nadine, Scheinberg, Anne (ed) (2001) *Integrated sustainable waste management (tools for decision makers-experiences from the Urban Waste Expertise Programme 1995-2001) Tool 5: The organic waste flow in integrated sustainable waste management* WASTE consultants, Urban Waste Expertise Programme (UWEP): WASTE: Gouda, the Netherlands

Eeghen, Marietje Van (1983) *The preparation and use of compost.* (Agrodok 8) Agromisa: Wageningen, Netherlands

EPA (1991). Environmental Fact Sheet - Yard Waste Composting, Environmental Protection Agency: Environmental Fact Sheet.

Epstein, E., Ed. (1997). The Science of Composting, Technomic Publishing Company.

Environmental Quality International (1983). The Market for Compost and Recovered Materials to be Produced by the Shoubra Composting Facility, Environmental Quality International. 177 pp.

European Commission (2000). Success stories on composting. Luxembourg, Office for Official Publications of the European Communities.

Evans, G. (1998). "Keeping Organics out of Landfills." BioCycle(October): 72-74.

Ewenkhare, E. O. (1984). A Study of the Introduction of Composting as an Alternative Means of Solid Waste Disposal in Shasha Settlement - Oyo State, University of Ibadan Nigeria. 121 pp.

FAO (un-dated) Soil management: compost production and use in tropical and subtropical environments, Food and Agriculture Organization of the United Nations Rome: FAO Soils Bulletin:: 56.

FAO (1975). FAO Soils Bulletin: Organic Materials as Fertilizers. Report of an Expert Consultation held in Rome, 2-6 December 1974. (FAO-SIDA), Food and Agriculture Organization of the United Nations Rome. 394 pp.

FAO (1977). FAO Soils Bulletin: China: Recycling of Organic Wastes in Agriculture. Report on a FAO/UNDP Study Tour to the People's Republic of China, 28 April-24 May 1977, Food and Agriculture Organization of the United Nations Rome. 107 pp.

FAO (1980). Compost Technology. Project Field Document No. 13. The collected lectures delivered during the project Training Course held at New

Delhi, India, October-November, 1980, Food and Agriculture Organization of the United Nations Rome (FAO/UNDP Regional Project RAS/75/004). 214 pp.

FAO (1981). Management of Organic Recycling. Proceedings of the Project Seminar held in Kathmandu, March 9-14, 1981. (FAO/UNDP Regional Project RAS/75/004), Food and Agriculture Organization of the United Nations Rome.

FAO (1982). FAO Agricultural Services Bulletin: Agricultural Residues: Bibliography 1975-1981 and Quantitative Survey, Food and Agriculture Organization of the United Nations Rome. 160 pp.

Farrel, M (2000) *Recovering costs of managing manure*. Journal article. Vermont, USA: Biocycle.

Favoino, E & Ragazzi, R (1998) *Italian organic recovery systems: Strategies and outcomes*. Article Scuola Agraria del Parco di Monza. Warmer Bulletin No 62. Residua Ltd, UK.

Fernandes, L., Sartaj, M. (1997). "Comparative Study of Static Pile Composting Using Natural, Forced and Passive Aeration Methods." Compost Science & Utilization 5(4): 65-77.

Gamage, W, Shaun, V & Outerbridge, T (1999) *Composting urban waste in Sri Lanka*. Article. Warmer Bulletin No.63: Residua Ltd, UK.

Gamage, W., Vincent, S., Outerbridge, T. (1998). "Composting Urban Waste in Sri Lanka." Appropriate Technology 25(No. 3).

Gardner, G. (1997). Recycling Organic Waste: From Urban Pollutant to Farm Resource. Worldwatch Paper 135.

Golueke, C. G. (1977). "The Biological Approach to Solid Waste Management." Compost Science.

Gotaas, Harold B (1956) *Composting sanitary disposal and reclamation of organic wastes: WHO monograph series No31* WHO: Geneva

Gonzalez del Carpio, C. (1998). "A New Approach - Composting has Promising Future in Mexico City." Biocycle, Journal of Waste Recycling(December): 76-77.

Grant, C.D (1978) *Health related aspects of solid waste management.* (Proceedings and papers of the 46th Annual Conference of the California Mosquito and Vector Control Association Inc. (Jan 29th-Feb 1st, 1978). Yosemite, California: CMVCA Press: Visalia, California, USA

Grist, B & Rogers M (1999) *Option choice for major waste management projects- two case studies.* Article. Municipal Engineer Volume ME133 Issue3: Institute of Civil Engineering (ICE), UK

GTZ, GFA-Umwelt, (1999). Decision Maker's Guide to Compost Production, Software Tool - Economic Model. Eschborn, GTZ.

GTZ & GFA-Umwelt (1999). Utilisation of organic waste in (peri-) urban centers. Eschborn, GTZ.

Gupta, D.N, (1992) *A report on New Delhi Municipal Committee's compost plant installed at Okhla, New Delhi, India* New Delhi Municipal Committee, India.

Halla, Francos & Majani, Bituro (1999) *Innovative ways for solid waste management in Dar-Es-Salaam.* Journal article. Habitat International Volume 23 No.3: Elsevier Science Ltd: Oxford, UK.

Hamoda, M. F., Qdais, H. A., Newham, J. (1998). "Evaluation of municipal solid waste composting kinetics." Resources, Conservation and Recycling 23: 209-223.

Hassen, A, Kaouala, Belguith, Jedidi, N, Cherif, M & Boudabous, A (2001) *Microbial characterisation during composting of municipal solid waste.* Journal article. Laboratoire Eau et Environment, Institut National de Recherche, Scientifique et Technique Tunis, Tunisia: Bioresource Technology.

Hassen, A., et al., (2001). "Microbial characterization during composting of municipal solid waste." Bioresource Technology(80): 217-225.

Haug, R.T (1980) *Compost Engineering: Principles and practices.* Ann Arbor Science Publishers, Inc. USA

Hay, J. C., Kuchenrither, R. D. (1990). "Fundamentals and application of windrow composting." Journal of Environmental Engineering 116(No.4): 746-763.

Hicklenton, P.R, Rodd, V, Warman, P.R (2001) *The effectiveness and consistency of source-separated Municipal Solid Waste and bark composts as components of container growing media.* Journal Article. Agriculture and Agri-Food Canada, Antlantic Food and Horticulture Research Centre, Nova Scotia, Canada: Scientia Horticulturae

Hogg, D. (2002). "Composting waste - assessing the costs and benefits." Waste Management World(March-April): 35-41.

Hoitink, H. A. J., Keener, H. M., Ed. (1993). Science and Engineering of Composting. Worthington, Renaissance Publications.

Hoornweg, D., Thomas, L., Otten, L. (1999). Composting and its applicability in developing countries, The World Bank.

Houck, N. J., Burckhart, E. P. (2001). "Penn State research uncovers Clopyralid in compost." Biocycle: 32.

Howard, A. (1933). "The Waste Products of Agriculture: Their Utilization as Humus." Journal of the Royal Society of Arts.

Human Resource Management & Development Corporation (HRMDC) (1996) *Solid waste management programme: in search of a better tomorrow* HMRDC: Peshawar

Hussain, T. (1994). "Effective Microorganisms." ILEIA Newsletter - for low and external input and sustainable agriculture vol 10(3): 15.

IBSRAM (2000). Co-composting of faecal sludge and municipal organic waste for urban and peri-urban agriculture. IBSRAM. Bangkok, Thailand, French Ministry of Foreign Affairs.

IETC Report 2, UNEP International Environmental Technology Centre (IETC)(1998) *Principals of municipal solid waste management: proceedings of a seminar implemented 21-24 October 1996 in Puerto Princesa, Philippines in collaboration with the City Government of Puerto Princessa, The league of cities of the Philippines and the International Solid Waste Association (ISWA).* IETC: Osaka/Shiga

IRCWD (1978). An Annotated Bibliography on Compost, Compost Quality and Composting, 1971-1977, Internat. Reference Centre for Waste Disposal. 400 pp.

Inckel, M., de Smet, P., Tersmette, T., Veldkamp T. (1990). The Preparation and Use of Compost, Agromisa Wageningen the Netherlands. 25 pp.

Inckel, M., et al., (1999). The preparation and use of compost, Technical center for Agricultural and Rural Cooperation (CTA).

Information Centre on Management and Utilization of Wastes (1989). Agricultural Waste Abstracts, University Pertanian Malaysia. 92 pp

International Energy Agency (IEA) Bioenergy Group (1998) *Anaerobic Digestion systems and markets*. Report. Warmer Bulletin No.61: Residua Ltd, UK

Jain, A.P (1994) *Solid waste Management in India*. Paper presented at the 20th WEDC Conference, Colombo Sri Lanka (G.B Pant institute of Himalayan Environment Development, India): WEDC, Loughborough University: Loughborough, UK.

Jain, A.P, Kuniyal, J.C & Shannigrahi, A.S (1996) *Solid waste management in Mohal (India)* Paper presented at the 22nd WEDC Conference, New Delhi, India: WEDC, Loughborough University: Loughborough, UK.

Jain, A.P, Dhawan, S, Chaudri, N.R, Shannigrahi, A & Ramanpreet (2000) *Solid waste management in Manali (India)*. Paper presented at the 26th WEDC Conference, Dhaka, Bangladesh: WEDC, Loughborough University: Loughborough UK.

Jalal, K. F. (1969). "A Technological Evaluation of Composting for Community Waste Disposal in Asia." Compost Science(Spring, Summer): 20 -25.

Jeong Y-K., K., J-S. (2001). "A new method for conservation of nitrogen in aerobic composting processes." Bioresource Technology 79: 129-133.

Jilani, S (2000) *Municipal solid wastes compost characteristics (Pakistan)*. Paper presented at the 26th WEDC Conference, Dhaka, Bangladesh: WEDC, Loughborough University: Loughborough UK.

J.G. Press Inc. (1996) *Biocycle- journal of composting and Recycling* J.G. Press Inc.

Kapanen, A & Itaevaara, M (1998) *Komposti ja Ekotoksikologia: Kirjallisuuskatsaus (Ecotoxicology and Composting. Literature Review)* Report. Valtion Teknillinen Tutkimuskeskus, Espoo (Finland). Biotechnology and Food Research. Sponsor: Technology Development Centre of Finland: Helsinki

Kaschl, A, Neumann, E, Chen, Y & Romheld, V (2001) *Agricultural application of Municipal Solid Waste compost in the Gaza Strip: Insitu measurement of nutrient and heavy metal leaching.* (Book chapter, conference paper) Plant Nutrition Colloquium, Hanover, Germany: Kluver Academic Publishers: Dordrecht, The Netherlands.

Kashmanian, R. M., Spencer, R. L. (1993). "Cost considerations of municipal sold waste compost - production versus market price." Compost Science & Utilization 1(1): 20-36.

Kehren, L &Vaillant, J (1963) *informatory report: household refuse processing and importance of aerobic composting in tropical environment* Central Bureau for the Study of Equipment for Overseas No 23, UK.

Kelleher, M (1997) *Source-separation of household organic waste delivers resources and landfill diversion: Canada.* Article. Warmer Bulletin No. 57: Residua Ltd, UK

Kielly, G (1997) *Environment Engineering.* Book. Pp 597-600 & 657-662:McGraw-Hill International (UK) Ltd.

Kitwana, M., Aveni, M., Adams, M. (1992). National Composting Program May 1992, United States Conference of Mayors: US Solid Waste Composting Facility Profiles.

Ladhar, Satnam S (1996) *Solid waste management in Punjab.* Paper presented at the 22nd WEDC Conference, New Delhi, India: WEDC, Loughborough University: Loughborough: Loughborough UK.

Landin, C. (1994). "Earthworms earn their credits." ILEIA Newsletter - for low and external input and sustainable agriculture vol 10(3): 9.

Lardinois, Inge & Van de Klundert, Arnold (1994) *Small-scale urban organic waste recovery*. Paper presented at the 20th WEDC Conference, Colombo Srilanka. (WASTE Consultants, The Netherlands): WEDC, Loughborough University: Loughborough, UK.

Lardinois, I., Marchand, R. (2000). Technical and Financial Evaluation of Composting Programmes in the Philippines, India, and Nepal. Internet Conference on Material Flow Analysis of Integrated Bio-Systems, Internet.

Lardinois, I., van de Klundert, A. (1993). Organic Waste - Options for small-scale resource recovery. Urban Solid Waste Series 1. Amsterdam, Tool Publications.

Lardinois, I., van de Klundert, A. (1994). "Recovery of organic wastes in cities." ILEIA Newsletter - for low and external input and sustainable agriculture vol 10(3): 4-5.

Lasaridi, K.E, Stentiford, E.I (2001) *Composting of source separated Municipal Solid Waste: an approach o respirometric techniques and biodegradation kinetics*. Journal article. Department of Geography, Harokopia University of Athens, Greece: Acta Horticulturae.

Lemmes, Bert (1999) *Sustainability is a frame of mind*. Article. International Directory of Solid Waste Management (ISWA) YearBook 1999/2000: James & James (Science Publishers): London, UK.

Lemmes, B. (1995). "The Challenge". Fitting Composting and Anaerobic Digestion into Integrated Waste Management. Proceedings. of the ORCA Congress. ORCA Congress, Sheraton Airport Hotel Brussels, Belgium.

Leton, T. G., Stentiford, E. I. (1990). "Control of Aeration in Static Pile Composting." Waste Management & Research(8): 299-306.

Lewcock C. (1995) *Farmer Use of Urban Waste in Kano*. Habitat International, vol. 19, no. 2, pp. 225-234(10) Elsevier Science

Lohani, B.N, Todino, G, Jindal, R. & Luduig, H.F (1984) *Recycling of solid wastes*. Environmental Sanitation Reviews No 13/14 1984. Environmental Sanitation Information Centre (ENSIC): Thailand

Maddox, J.J., Almond, R.A., Broder, M.F., Hoagland, J.J. & Kelly, DA (1998) *Results of a Study Investigating the Plant Uptake of Explosive Residues From Compost of Explosives-Contaminated Soil Obtained from the Umatilla Army Depot Activity*. Tennessee Valley Authority, Muscle Shoals, AL.

Madrid, F, Murillo, J.M, Lopez, R & Cabrera, F (2000) *Use of urea to correct immature urban composts for agriculture purposes*. (Journal article). Instuto de recursos Naturales y Agrobilologia CSIC, Sevilla, Spain: Communication in Soil Science & Plant Analysis.

Mamo, M, Monncrief, J.F, Rosen, C.J & Halbach, T.R (2000) *the effect of municipal solid waste compost application on soil water and water stress in irrigated corn*. (Journal article) Department of Soil, Water, and Climate, University of Minnesota, Minnesota, USA: Compost Science & Utilization.

Marcote, I, Hernandez, T &Garcia, C (2001) *Influence of one or two successive annual applications of organic fertilisers on the enzyme activity of a soil under barley cultivation*. (Journal article).Centro de Ciencias Medioambientales (CSIC) Madrid, Spain: Bioresource Technology.

Marmo, L (1998) *Organic waste treatment in Europe*. Conference report. European Commissions Directorate-general XI. Warmer Bulletin No.61. . Residua Ltd, UK.

Mata- Alvarez, J, et al. (1999) Anaerobic digestion. University of Barcelona, Spain. Article. Warmer Bulletin No.69: Residua Ltd, UK.

Marriott, J. The Commercial Production of Organic Materials for Soil Improvement in Developing Countries, United Nations Industrial Development Organization. 30 pp.

Matsumoto, J., Matsuo, T. (1986). Treatment, Disposal and Management of Human Wastes. Proceedings of an IAWPRC Conference. Iawprc, Tokyo, Japan, Pergamon Press Oxford New York.

Mazumdar, I & Mazumdar, N.B (1997) *Domestic rapid composter*. International Institute of Technical Research. Funded by Indian Department of Science and Technology. (Article). Warmer Bulletin No. 56: Residua Ltd, UK.

McDougal, F, & Fonteyne, J (1999) European waste management systems: Case studies & lessons learned. Article. Warmer Bulletin: Residua Ltd, UK

McGarry, M.G, & Stainforth, J (1978), *Compost, fertilizer and Biogas production from human and farm wastes in the People's Republic of China* IDRCT TS 8 e, International Development Research Centre (IDRCT): Canada

McLeod, C. A., Terazawa, M., Yamamura, E. (1997). "Using geographical information systems to evaluate decentralized manaagment of municipal food waste." Compost Science & Utilization 5(1): 49-61.

McGowin, A.E, Adom, K.K &Abubuafo, A.K (2001) *Screening of compost for Polycyclic Aromatic Hydrocarbons (PAH) and pesticides using static sub-critical water extraction.* Journal article. Department of chemistry, Wright State University, Dayton, Ohio, USA: Chemosphere.

Miller, FC; Clark, T (1998) *Literature review and position paper on composting as a method of remediating petroleum contaminated soils*: Final report Alberta Environmental Protection, Edmonton

Miller, M. (2001). "Fullfilling Special Needs of Nurseries." Biocycle(3): 55-58.

Moorman, T.B, Cowan, J.K, Arthur, E.L &Coats, J.R (2001) *Organic amendments to enhance herbicide biodegradation in contaminated soils.* (Journal article) USDA-ARS, National Soil Tilth Laboratory, Ames, USA: Biology & Fertility of Soils.

Morris, J.R (2000) *Composting livestock mortalities Ontario.* Agriculture & Rural Division: Guelph, Ontario

Murphy, R. J., Brennan, T. J. (1992). Aerobic Degradation of Municipal Solid Waste. 85th Annual Meeting & Exhibition of the Air and Waste Management Association, Kansas City, Missouri.

Muwic (1989). Agricultural Waste Abstracts, Information Centre on Management and Utilization of Wastes (MUWIC) University Pertanian Malaysia. 92 pp.

Namkoong, W., Hwang, E-Y. (1997). "Operational Parameters for Composting Nightsoil in Korea." Compost Science & Utilization 5(4): 46-51.

115

Natural Resources, Agriculture and Engineering Services (NRAES) (2001) *Farm based composting: Manure and more* (38 min. video) Cornell Waste Management Institute: Cornell University: Ithaca, NY

Negro, M.J., Solano, M.L., Carrasco, J. & Ciria, P. (1998) *Sweet Sorghum crop. Effect of the Compost Application.* Centro de Investigaciones Energeticas, Medioambientalesy tecnologicas (CIEMAT): Madrid, Spain

Neogi, S.K, & Mukherjee, S.K (2000) *Recycling Municipal solid wastes (India).* Paper presented at the 26th WEDC Conference, Dhaka, Bangladesh: WEDC, Loughborough University: Loughborough UK.

Newport, H.A, Bardos, R.P, Hensler, K, Goss, E, Willet, S, King, P, & Warren Spring Laboratory (1993) *The technical aspects of controlled waste management: Municipal waste composting.* Department of the Environment Report No. CWM/074/93, File 174/04 LR937.Department of the Environment, Wastes Technical Division: London

Nicolaisen, D.et al.(undated) *Solid waste management with people's participation- an example in Nepal.* GTZ publication No231. GTZ: Eschborn, Germany.

Nicolaisen, D., Spreen, E. (1991). Evaluation of Alternative Compost Production Concepts - Pre-Feasibility Study (Nepal, Kathmandu), GTZ Deutsche Gesellschaft für Technische Zusammenarbeit Eschborn S.W.M.R.M.C. Solid Waste Management & Resource Mobilization Centre Kathmandu Nepal. ca. 80 pp.

Nieveen, Onno (1999) *Composting in the new Millennium: An overview*: Article. International Directory of Solid Waste Management (ISWA) YearBook 1999/ 2000: James & James (Science Publishers) Ltd: London, UK.

Nissim, I, Evan, M, Even-Danan, R, Gonen-Livne, O & Gabbay (1999) *Waste management in Israel.* Ministry of the Environment. Article. Warmer Bulletin: Residua Ltd, UK

Nova Scotia. Dept. of the Environment (1998) *composting facility guidelines* Nova Scotia. Dept. of the Environment, Halifax.

Nunan, Fiona (2000) *Urban organic waste markets: responding to change in Hubli-Dharwad, India.* (Journal article) Habitat International Volume 23 No.3: Elsevier Science Ltd, Oxford, UK.

Nunan, F, Brook, R, Chandra, H & Shindhe, K (2000) Waste not want not: Making most of urban organic waste. International Development Department, University of Birmingham: Birmingham, UK.

Obeng, L.A., & Wright, F.W. (1987) *The composting of domestic solid and human waste* The World Bank, Technology Advisory Group: Washington, D.C

Obeng, L. A., Wright, F. W. (1987). Integrated Resource Recovery. The Co-Composting of Domestic Solid and Human Wastes, The World Bank Washington + UNDP. 101 pp.

ORCA (1992). Information on Composting and Anaerobic Digestion., Organic Reclamation & Composting Association: ORCA Technical Publication: Nr. 1. 74 pp.

ORCA (1995). The challenge - fitting composting and anaerobic digestion into integrated waste management. Proceedings of the ORCA Comgress, Brussels, Belgium, 18-19 January 1995, Organic Reclamation & Composting Association.

Ouédraogo, E., Mando, A., Zombré, N. P. (2001). "Use of compost to improve soild properties and crop productivity under low input agricultural system in West Africa." Agriculture, Ecosystems and Environment 84: 259-266.

Owens, V.N & Doolittle, J.J (2000) *Establish Alfalfa on high clay soils after application of municipal solid waste.* Proceeding/reports of the American Forage and Grassland Council, 37th North American Alfalfa improvement Conference, Madison, Winconsin, July 16-19, 2000: American Forage and Grassland Council: Georgetown, USA.

Owusu-Bennoah, V., C. (1994). "Organic waste hijacked." ILEIA Newsletter - for low and external input and sustainable agriculture vol 10(3): 12-13.

Olokowookere, A.O, Coker, A.O & Shridhar, M.K.C (2001) *Gender involvement in community wastes management in urban Nigeria.* Paper presented at the 27th WEDC Conference, Lusaka, Zambia: WEDC, Loughborough University: Loughborough, UK.

Ott, D.K (2001) *Evaluation of Occupational Exposures at Compost Production Facilities.* Performer: Air Force Institute of Technology, Wright-Patterson AFB: Ohio, USA

Panduan Praktis Pembuatan Kompos (Practical Handbook on Composting). Jakarta, Centre for Policy and Implementation Studies (CPIS) and Harvard Institute for International Development (HIID).

Pereira-Neto, J. T. (2001). "Controlled Composting in Developing Countries." Biocycle(2): 84-86.

Poorbaugh, J.H, & Diener, R.G (ed) (1993) *Composting of solid waste in West Virginia.* (Journal article) West Virginia Agricultural and Forestry Experiment Station: West Virginia University, Morgan town, West Virginia, USA

Rao, B. S., Ranade, S. V., Gadgil, J. M. (1995). Wealth from Waste - Fertilizer from Spentwash. 3rd International Conference on Appropriate Waste Management Technologies for Developing Countries, Nagpur, India.

Riggle, D (1999) *Breaking down the future - Biodegradable plastics for waste management.* Article. Warmer BulletinNo.65: Residua Ltd, UK.

Rivard, C.J, Duff, B.W, Dickow, J.H, Wiles, C.C, Nagle, N.J, Gaddy, J.L, & Clausen, E.C (1998) *Demonstration evaluation of a novel high solids anaerobic digestion process for converting organic wastes to fuel gas and compost.* (Journal article) Pinnacle Biotechnologies International Inc, Colorado, USA: Applied Biochemistry.

Rosario, Anselm (1994). *Decentralised solid waste management approach.* Paper presented at the 20th WEDC Conference, Colombo, Sri Lanka: WEDC, Loughborough University: Loughborough, UK.

Roulac, John (1999) *Backyard composting* Straight Recycling Systems: Green Books: Totnes, Devon

Satis (1983). The Philippines Recommend for FERTILIZER USAGE. Science & Appropriate Technology Information Services, SATIS Technology Information Network Batangas City Philippines. 103.

Selvam, Paneer (1994) *Community based solid waste project preparation.* Paper presented at the 20th WEDC Conference, Colombo, Sri Lanka: WEDC, Loughborough University: Loughborough, UK.

Sequi, P. (1997). The role of composting in sustainable agriculture. The Science of Composting. E. Epstein, Technomic Publishing Company.

Seung-Mok, K. (1995). Demand and Supply of Waste-Derived Compost in Bangkok Metropolitan Region, Thailand. Thesis for MS Degree, Asian Institute of Technology Bangkok Thailand: 144 pp.

Shukla, S.R (1992) *Solid waste management - Indian scenario* Paper presented at the 18th WEDC Conference, Kathmandu, Nepal: WEDC, Loughborough University: Loughborough, UK

Simpson-Herbert, Mayling, Wood, Sara (eds) (1998) *Sanitation promotion (WHO/EOS/98.5)* Water Supply and Sanitation Collaborative Council (WSSCC), WSSCC Working Group on Promotion of Sanitation: WHO: Geneva

Slater, R.A & Frederickson, J (2001) *Composting of Municipal waste in the UK: some lessons from Europe.* Journal article. Integrated Waste Systems, The Open University Milton Keynes, UK: Resource Conservation and Recycling.

Slater, R. A., Frederickson, J. (2001). "Composting municipal waste in the UK: some lessons from Europe." Resources, Conservation and Recycling 32.

Smith, O. B., Ed. (1999). Urban Agriculture in West Africa - Contributing to Food Security and Urban Sanitation, IDRC.

Snel, M (1999) *Community composting and vermiculture.* Journal article. WEDC, Loughborough University, UK: Appropriate technology

Snel, M (1999) *Community based vermicomposting in developing countries.* Journal article. WEDC, Loughborough University, UK: Biocycle.

Sonesson, U., Björklund, A., Carlson, M., Dalemo, M. (2000). Economic analysis of options for managing biodegradable municipal wastes: Overview of Ongoing work for the EC.

Sonesson, U., Björklund, A., Carlson, M., Dalemo, M. (2000). "Environmental and economic analysis of management systems for biodegradable wastes." Resources, Conservation and Recycling (28).

Stentiford, E.I, (1991) *Composting of sewage sludges and solid wastes.* Report. Unpublished.

Stentiford, E.I, Pereira Neto, J.T & Mara, D.D (1996) *Low cost composting.* University of Leeds: Leeds

Stentiford, E. I., Pereira Neto, J. T., Mara, D. D. (1996). Low cost composting. Leeds, University of Leeds.

Stofella, P.J, Ozores-Hampton, M, & Patterson, D.T (2000) *Potential of Municipal Solid Waste Compost as a biological weed control.* (Journal article): Acta Horticulturae.

Thanga, V.S.G & Ramaswani, P.P (2000) *Dynamics of heavy metals in soil as influenced by solid waste application.* (Journal article) Department of Environmental Science, Tamil Nadu Agricultural University, India: Journal of Ecotoxicology & Environmental Monitoring.

Thapa, Gopal B (1998) *Lessons learned from solid waste management in Kathmandu, Nepal.* (Journal article) Habitat International Volume 22 No. 2

The Environment Council (2000) *Waste Type: Organic and Food.* Article. The stakeholders' Guide for sustainable waste management: The Environment Council 2000: London, UK.

The Swedish Environment Protection Agency (EPA) (1999) *Waste management- A Swedish model.* Article. Warmer Bulletin No 66: Residua Ltd, UK

The UK Composting Association (1998) *Composting.* Article. Warmer Bulletin No.60. Residua Ltd, UK. Warmer Bulletin No.59. Residua Ltd, UK.

Thi Huong, L. (1995). Urban Waste-Derived Compost in Hanoi, Vietnam: Factors Affecting Supply and Demand. Thesis for MS Degree, Asian Institute of Technology Bangkok Thailand: 136 pp.

Tyler, R. W. (1996). Winning the organics game - the compost marketers handbook. Alexandria, ASHS Press.

UK Department of the Environment (1991) Recycling. Waste management paper No.28. Crown copyright, UK

UK Department of the Environment (1992) A review of options. Waste management paper No.1. First published 1976. Crown copyright, UK

UK Department of the Environment & the Environment Agency (1997) *Markets and quality requirements for compost*. Article. Warmer Bulletin No. 56. Residua Ltd, UK.

University of Saskatchewan. Department of Agricultural & Bioresource Engineering (2001) *Evaluation and demonstration of composting as an option for dead animal management in Saskatchewan: Final report* Agriculture Development Fund, Canada.

Urban Waste Expertise Programme (UWEP), Hart, Doortje't, Pluijmers, Jacomijn & WASTE Consultants (1996) *Wasted agriculture: the use of compost in urban agriculture*. UWEP Working Document 1. WASTE: Gouda, The Netherlands

US Environment Protection Agency (EPA) (1999) *Municipal solid waste in the US*. Article. Warmer Bulletin No.69: Residua Ltd, UK.

US Environment Protection Agency (EPA) (1999) don't throw away that food: Strategies for record setting waste reduction. Article. Warmer Bulletin No.66: Residua Ltd, UK

US Environment Protection Agency (USEPA) (1999) don't throw away that food: Strategies for record setting waste reduction. Article. Warmer Bulletin No.66: Residua Ltd, UK

US Environment Protection Agency (EPA) & Solid waste and Emergency Response (1989) *Decision makers guide to solid waste management (Report No EPA/530-SW-89-072)* EPA: Solid Waste Emergency Response: Washington, D.C

US Environment Protection Agency (EPA) & Solid waste and Emergency Response (1994) *Waste prevention, recycling and composting options: lessons from 30 communities (EPA 530-R-92-015)* EPA: Solid Waste Emergency Response: Washington, D.C

US Environment Protection Agency (EPA), Municipal and Industrial Solid Waste Division Office of Solid waste (1991) *Environment Fact sheet: yard waste composting.* EPA: http://www.epa.gov/epaoswer/osw/non-hw/compost (14th May 2002)

US Environment Protection Agency (EPA), Solid Waste & Emergency Response (1994) *Waste prevention, recycling and composting Lessons from 30 communities.* EPA: http://www.epa.gov/epaoswer/osw/non-hw/compost (14th May 2002)

US Environment Protection Agency (EPA), Solid Waste & Emergency Response (1999) *Organic materials management strategies.* EPA: http://www.epa.gov/epaoswer/osw/non-hw/compost (14th May 2002)

US Environment Protection Agency (EPA), Solid Waste & Emergency Response (1992) *Environment Fact sheet: Recycling grass clippings.* EPA: http://www.epa.gov/epaoswer/osw/non-hw/compost (14th May 2002)

US Environment Protection Agency (EPA), Solid Waste & Emergency Response (1999) *The effect of composted organic materials on the growth factors for hard wood and softwood. Tree seedlings.* EPA: http://www.epa.gov/epaoswer/osw/non-hw/compost (14th May 2002)

US Environment Protection Agency (EPA), Solid Waste & Emergency Response (1996) *The consumer's handbook for reducing solid waste.* EPA: http://www.epa.gov/epaoswer/non-hw/reduce/catbook (14th May 2002)

US Environment Protection Agency (EPA), Solid Waste & Emergency Response (1994) Composting of yard trimmings and municipal solid waste. EPA: http://www.epa.gov/epaoswer/non-hw/compost/cytmsw.pdf (14th May 2002)

US Environment Protection Agency (EPA), Solid Waste & Emergency Response (1999) *Biosolids generation, use and the disposal in the United States.* EPA: http://www.epa.gov/epaoswer/non-hw/compost/biosolids.pdf (14th May 2002)

US Environment Protection Agency (EPA), Municipal and Industrial waste Division (1998) *An analysis of composting as an environment remediation technology.* EPA: http://www.epa.gov/epaoswer/non-hw/compost/index.htm (14th May 2002)

US Environment Protection Agency (EPA), Solid Waste & Emergency Response (1998) *Innovative uses of compost: Reforestation, wetlands restoration and habitat revitalization.* EPA: http://epa.gov/epaoswer/non-hw/compost (14th May 2002)

US Environment Protection Agency (EPA), Solid Waste & Emergency Response (1998) *Innovative uses of compost: Composting of soil contaminated by explosives.* EPA: http://epa.gov/epaoswer/non-hw/compost (14th May 2002)

US Environment Protection Agency (EPA), Solid Waste & Emergency Response (1997) *Innovative uses of compost: Erosion control, turf remediation and landscaping.* EPA: http://epa.gov/epaoswer/non-hw/compost (14th May 2002)

US Environment Protection Agency (EPA), Solid Waste & Emergency Response (1997) *Innovative uses of compost: Disease control for plants and animals.* EPA: http://epa.gov/epaoswer/non-hw/compost (14th May 2002)

US Environment Protection Agency (EPA), Solid Waste & Emergency Response (1997) *Innovative uses of compost: Bioremediation and pollution prevention.* EPA: http://epa.gov/epaoswer/non-hw/compost (14th May 2002)

Waste watch(2002) Centralised community composting. http://www.watewatch.org.uk/informtn/compost.htm (5th May 2002)

Waste Watch (2002) *Examples of community composting schemes.* http://www.watewatch.org.uk/informtn/compost.htm. (5th May 2002)

Waste Watch (2002) *How to make a worm composter.* http://www.wastewatch.org.uk/school-k/worm-bin.htm (5th May 2002)

Waste Watch (2002) *No wastage of money: How recycling can be funded.* http://www.wastewatch.org.uk/r-and-p/resea/ (5th May 02)

Warmer Bulletin (1997) *Biological waste treatment: news from around the world.* Article. Warmer Bulletin No. 57: Residua Ltd, UK.

Warmer Bulletin (1998) *Composting with worms.* Information sheet. Warmer Bulletin No.60. Residua Ltd, UK.

Warmer Bulletin (1997) *Organic waste treatment: Composting in rural France.* Article. Warmer Bulletin No. 56: Residua Ltd, UK.

Weerasinghe, T.J & Ratnayake, N (1994) *Composting of municipal solid waste.* Paper presented at the 20th WEDC Conference, Colombo, Sri Lanka: WEDC, Loughborough University: Loughborough, UK.

Wei, Y.-S., Fan, Y-B., Wang, M-J., Wang, J-S. (2000). "Composting and compost application in China." Resources, Conservation and Recycling 30: 277-300.

Wheeler, P (2000) *commercial and strategic perspectives for anaerobic digestion.* Article. International Directory of Waste Management (ISWA) YearBook 2000/2001: James and James (Science Publishers) Ltd, London, UK.

Yousuf, Tariq Bin (2000) *Community wastes management-possibilities of partnership in Bangladesh.* Paper presented at the 26th WEDC Conference, Dhaka, Bangladesh: WEDC, Loughborough University, UK.

Zachary, J., Shiralipour, A. (1994). Santa Barbara County - Preliminary Compost Market Assessment. Santa Barbara, Environmental Council Inc., Gildea Resource Center, California Integrated Waste Management Board: Report. 42.

Zhang, M, Heaney, D, Solberg, E & Heriquez (2000) *The effect of MSW (municipal solid waste) compost on metal uptake and yield of wheat barley and canola in less productive farming soils of Alberta.* (Journal article) Agronomy Unit, Alberta Agriculture, Food and Rural Development Alberta, Canada: Compost Science and Utilization.

Zoethout, T (2000) *Digestion goes Dutch: Anaerobic Digestion converts city waste to energy.* Article. International Directory of Waste Management (ISWA) YearBook 2000/2001: James and James (Science Publishers) Ltd, London, UK.

Zurbrugg, C., Aristanti, C. (1999). "Resource Recovery in a Primary Collection Scheme in Indonesia." SANDEC News(No. 4).